cook's library
Soups

p

This is a Parragon Publishing Book
This edition published in 2003

Parragon Publishing
Queen Street House
4 Queen Street
Bath BA1 1HE, UK

Copyright © Parragon 2002

ISBN: 0-75259-955-0

Printed in China

NOTE

Cup measurements in this book are for American cups. This book
uses imperial and metric measurements. Follow the same units of
measurement throughout; do not mix imperial and metric. All spoon
measurements are level: teaspoons are assumed to be 5 ml,
and tablespoons are assumed to be 15 ml. Unless otherwise stated,
milk is assumed to be full fat, eggs and individual vegetables such
as potatoes are medium, and pepper is freshly ground black pepper.

The times given for each recipe are an approximate guide only because
the preparation times may differ according to the techniques used by
different people and the cooking times may vary as a result of the type
of oven used. The preparation times include chilling and marinating
times, where appropriate.

Recipes using raw or very lightly cooked eggs should be avoided
by infants, the elderly, pregnant women, convalescents, and anyone
suffering from an illness.

Contents

Introduction

Soup is one of the most fundamental forms of food. Its traditions go back to the earliest days of civilized man with the advent of fire. It remains a favorite source of nourishment and pleasure today and homemade soup has become a special treat.

The benefits of soup are numerous. It is nutritious, satisfying to eat, and generally lean. It is economical to make, especially using abundant seasonal produce, but even expensive ingredients like lobster go further when made into soups.

Making soup can be a very creative endeavor, as satisfying for the cook as the recipients. Practice hones skills and promotes confidence. This book offers an array of different styles of soup, using a variety of ingredients and techniques. Consider the recipes as a framework of proportions, and experiment with alternative ingredients if you wish.

Ingredients

Soups are as good as the ingredients in them. While leftovers have traditionally been a springboard for creativity in soup-making, and may certainly provide useful components, fresh ingredients at their peak provide optimum nutritional benefits and taste. Water is the most basic ingredient for soup. Even stock is essentially flavored water. Many soups taste best made with water, as the pure flavors are highlighted; this is especially true of vegetable soups.

Some soups make their own stock during the cooking process. Others call for stock as an ingredient. This can be homemade, bought ready-made, made up from bouillon cubes, powder or liquid stock base, or canned consommé or clear broth. It is useful to know how to make stock, as homemade is more economical and normally has superior flavor.

Equipment

Soup-making requires little in the way of basic equipment. A good knife or two and a large saucepan with a lid are essential. A stock pot or soup kettle, or a large cast-iron casserole, is also useful. Other things needed to expedite your efforts are probably already in your kitchen—a cutting board, colander, strainers, vegetable peeler, scissors, ladle, spoons. A fat separator or de-greasing pitcher is helpful, as is a large measuring cup.

A wide range of specialized equipment is available, but not necessarily essential for making soups. For puréeing soups, the various options produce differing results. A food mill, the most economical choice, will do the basic job of producing relatively smooth soups and it also strains at the same time. For the smoothest and best texture, nothing beats a blender. A food processor may be used for chopping and slicing ingredients as well as puréeing cooked soups, so it performs a variety of functions. A hand-held blender can purée right in the saucepan, as long as the depth of liquid is appropriate.

These pieces of equipment may each have a role to play in soup-making, but it's best to experiment first and see what you really need for the soups you like to make before investing. For most people, there is no need for a battery of equipment. Always follow manufacturer's instructions and recommendations for safe operation of electric appliances.

Making Bouillon

Making bouillon is easy. After getting it under way, it requires little attention, just time. You can save bouillon ingredients in the freezer until you need them: chicken carcasses, giblets, necks, backs, and trimmings; scraps and bones from meat roasts; vegetable trimmings such as leek greens, celery leaves and stalks, mushroom stalks, pieces of carrot, and unused onion halves.

Recipes appear throughout the book using Fish Bouillon (see page 14), Beef Bouillon (see page 15), Chicken Bouillon (see page 14), and Vegetable Bouillon (see page 14). The following general points cover the basic techniques of making bouillon.

Fresh ingredients are determined by the kind of bouillon you want. Chicken or turkey wings are inexpensive and provide excellent flavor for poultry bouillon. Veal bones give more flavor than beef and pork bones lend sweetness. Lamb or ham bones are not suitable for a general purpose meat bouillon, as the flavors are too pronounced, but can make delicious bouillons when their flavors are appropriate, such as ham bouillon for split pea or bean soup. Aromatic vegetables—carrot, onion, leek, garlic, for instance—are almost always included in bouillon. Strongly flavored vegetables like cabbage or rutabaga should be used sparingly, as the bouillon produced would be unsuitable for delicate soups. Avoid dark greens as they make bouillon murky.

Except when a pale, delicate bouillon is wanted, browning the main ingredients first, either by roasting or sautéing, adds color and richer flavor to the bouillon. Adding a roast chicken carcass or two is an easy way to do this.

Use cold water to make bouillon; it helps extract impurities. For a flavorful bouillon, keep the amount of water in proportion to the ingredients, which should be covered by about 2 inches/5 cm. Skim off the scum or foam that rises to the surface as bouillon is heated, as it contains impurities that can make bouillon cloudy. Cook bouillon uncovered and do not allow it to boil at any point or fat may be incorporated into the liquid, unable to be removed.

Bouillon needs slow cooking over a low heat. Beef or meat bouillon takes 4–6 hours to extract maximum flavor, chicken or other poultry bouillon 2–3 hours. Fish bouillon only requires about half an hour .

Remove the fat from bouillon before using. The easiest way to do this is to refrigerate it, allowing the fat to congeal, then lift off the fat. If time is short, use a fat separator (a pitcher with the spout at the bottom) to remove the fat from warm bouillon, or spoon off the fat, although that is not nearly as effective as the other methods.

For greater flavor, bouillon can be reduced—cooked slowly, uncovered, to reduce and concentrate it. This procedure may also be useful to reduce the volume for storage. Stock keeps refrigerated for about 3 days or frozen for several months.

Serving soup

Soup is more flexible in terms of portions than many other foods. In this book a range of servings may be indicated, as a soup will provide more servings as a starter than as the focus of a meal. Starter portions range from 1 cup for a very rich soup to $1\frac{1}{2}$ cups; main course portions from $1\frac{2}{3}$ cups to about $2\frac{1}{2}$ cups.

Soup is a perfect food for almost any occasion, from the most casual to the very formal. It can set the tone for the rest of a meal or be the meal itself. It brings satisfaction to those who make it as well as those who eat it and nourishes both the body and the soul.

Basic Recipes

These recipes form the basis of several of the dishes contained throughout this book. Many of these basic recipes can be made in advance and stored in the refrigerator until required.

Fresh Chicken Bouillon

MAKES
1¾ QUARTS

2 lb 4 oz/1 kg chicken, skinned
2 celery stalks, chopped
1 onion, sliced
2 carrots, chopped
1 garlic clove
few sprigs of fresh parsley
2 quarts water
salt and pepper

1 Place all the ingredients in a large pan and bring to a boil.

2 Skim away any surface scum using a large flat spoon. Reduce the heat to a gentle simmer, partially cover, and cook for 2 hours. Let cool.

3 Line a strainer with clean cheesecloth and place over a large pitcher or bowl. Pour the bouillon through the strainer. The cooked chicken can be used in another recipe. Discard the other solids. Cover the bouillon and chill.

4 Skim away any surface fat before using. Store in the refrigerator for up to 3 days, or freeze in small batches until required.

Fresh Vegetable Bouillon

MAKES
1¾ QUARTS

1 large onion, sliced
1 large carrot, chopped
1 celery stalk, chopped
2 garlic cloves
1 dried bay leaf
few sprigs of fresh parsley
pinch of grated nutmeg
2 quarts water
salt and pepper

1 Place all the ingredients in a large pan and bring to a boil.

2 Skim away any surface scum using a large flat spoon. Reduce the heat to a gentle simmer, partially cover, and cook for 45 minutes. Let cool.

3 Line a strainer with clean cheesecloth and place over a large pitcher or bowl. Pour the bouillon through the strainer. Discard the solids.

4 Cover the bouillon and store in the refrigerator for up to 3 days, or freeze in small batches.

Fresh Fish Bouillon

MAKES
1¾ QUARTS

2 lb 4 oz/1 kg white fish bones, heads, and scraps
1 large onion, chopped
2 carrots, chopped
2 celery stalks, chopped
½ tsp black peppercorns
½ tsp grated lemon zest
few sprigs of fresh parsley
2 quarts water
salt and pepper

1 Rinse the fish trimmings in cold water, place in a large pan with the other ingredients and bring to a boil.

2 Skim away any surface scum with using a large flat spoon. Reduce the heat to a gentle simmer, partially cover, and cook for 30 minutes. Let cool.

3 Line a strainer with clean cheesecloth and place over a large pitcher or bowl. Pour the bouillon through the strainer. Discard the solids.

4 Cover the bouillon and store in the refrigerator for up to 3 days, or freeze in small batches.

Fresh Chicken Bouillon

MAKES
1¾ QUARTS

2 lb 4 oz/1 kg chicken, skinned
2 celery stalks, chopped
1 onion, sliced
2 carrots, chopped
1 garlic clove
few sprigs of fresh parsley
2 quarts water
salt and pepper

1 Place all the ingredients in a large pan and bring to a boil.

2 Skim away any surface scum using a large flat spoon. Reduce the heat to a gentle simmer, partially cover, and cook for 2 hours. Let cool.

3 Line a strainer with clean cheesecloth and place over a large pitcher or bowl. Pour the bouillon through the strainer. The cooked chicken can be used in another recipe. Discard the other solids. Cover the bouillon and chill.

4 Skim away any surface fat before using. Store in the refrigerator for up to 3 days, or freeze in small batches until required.

Fresh Vegetable Bouillon

MAKES
1¾ QUARTS

1 large onion, sliced
1 large carrot, chopped
1 celery stalk, chopped
2 garlic cloves
1 dried bay leaf
few sprigs of fresh parsley
pinch of grated nutmeg
2 quarts water
salt and pepper

1 Place all the ingredients in a large pan and bring to a boil.

2 Skim away any surface scum using a large flat spoon. Reduce the heat to a gentle simmer, partially cover, and cook for 45 minutes. Let cool.

3 Line a strainer with clean cheesecloth and place over a large pitcher or bowl. Pour the bouillon through the strainer. Discard the solids.

4 Cover the bouillon and store in the refrigerator for up to 3 days, or freeze in small batches.

Fresh Fish Bouillon

MAKES
1¾ QUARTS

2 lb 4 oz/1 kg white fish bones, heads, and scraps
1 large onion, chopped
2 carrots, chopped
2 celery stalks, chopped
½ tsp black peppercorns
½ tsp grated lemon zest
few sprigs of fresh parsley
2 quarts water
salt and pepper

1 Rinse the fish trimmings in cold water, place in a large pan with the other ingredients and bring to a boil.

2 Skim away any surface scum using a large flat spoon. Reduce the heat to a gentle simmer, partially cover, and cook for 30 minutes. Let cool.

3 Line a strainer with clean cheesecloth and place over a large pitcher or bowl. Pour the bouillon through the strainer. Discard the solids.

4 Cover the bouillon and store in the refrigerator for up to 3 days, or freeze in small batches.

How to Use This Book

Each recipe contains a wealth of useful information, including a breakdown

of nutritional quantities, preparation and cooking times, and level of difficulty.

All of this information is explained in detail below.

A full-color photograph of the finished dish.

The ingredients for each recipe are listed in the order that they are used.

The nutritional information provided for each recipe is per serving or per portion. Optional ingredients, variations or serving suggestions have not been included in the calculations.

The method is clearly explained with step-by-step instructions that are easy to follow.

Cook's tips provide useful information regarding ingredients or cooking techniques.

The number of stars represents the difficulty of each recipe, ranging from very easy (1 star) to challenging (4 stars).

This amount of time represents the preparation of ingredients, including cooling, chilling, and soaking times.

This represents the cooking time.

Vegetable Soups

Vegetables offer an enormous range of options for making soups. Often the simplest soups to make, they also provide the most versatility. Think of each vegetable as the growing season unfolds and the innumerable ways each can be used in soups—creamy soups, broths, chunky soups, thick, and hearty soups. Vegetables provide simple nourishment or dramatic complexity, pure flavors or fascinating amalgamations, lean and healthy alliances or rich, tempting combinations.

Vegetable soups are endlessly variable and eminently enjoyable—and often beautifully colored, as well. They can provide a light starter to introduce a meal or a hearty and satisfying main course. While most soups are suitable for preparing ahead, vegetable soups are usually quickly cooked and often keep longer than other soups.

This soup, made with fresh tomatoes, tastes of summer, although it can be made at any time of year as long as the tomatoes are ripe.

Fresh Tomato Soup

SERVES 4

2 lb/900 g ripe plum tomatoes, peeled
2 tsp olive oil
1 large sweet onion, chopped finely
1 carrot, chopped finely
1 celery stalk, chopped finely
2 garlic cloves, chopped finely or crushed
2 sprigs fresh marjoram, or ¼ tsp dried marjoram
2 cups water
4–5 tbsp heavy cream, plus extra to garnish
2 tbsp chopped fresh basil leaves
salt and pepper

NUTRITION

Calories 254; Sugars 13 g; Protein 3 g; Carbohydrate 14 g; Fat 21 g; Saturates 10 g

  moderate

  10 mins

  1 hr

1 Cut the tomatoes in half and scrape the seeds into a strainer set over a bowl to catch the juice. Reserve the juice and discard the seeds. Chop the tomato flesh into large chunks.

2 Heat the olive oil in a large pan. Add the onion, carrot, and celery and cook over medium-low heat for 3–4 minutes, stirring occasionally.

3 Add the tomatoes and their juice, with the garlic and marjoram. Cook for 2 minutes. Stir in the water, reduce the heat, and simmer, covered, for about 45 minutes or until the vegetables are very soft, stirring occasionally.

4 Let the soup cool slightly, then transfer to a blender or food processor and purée until smooth, working in batches, if necessary. (If using a food processor, strain off the cooking liquid and reserve. Purée the soup solids with enough cooking liquid to moisten them, then combine with the remaining liquid.)

5 Return the soup to the pan and place over medium-low heat. Add the cream and stir in the basil. Season with salt and pepper and heat through; do not let boil.

6 Ladle the soup into warmed bowls and swirl a little extra cream into each serving. Serve at once.

A deep red soup makes a stunning first course—and it's easy in the microwave. A swirl of sour cream gives a very pretty effect.

Potato *and* Beet Soup

1 Place the onion, potatoes, apple, and water in a large bowl. Cover and cook in the microwave on High power for 10 minutes.

2 Stir in the cumin seeds and cook on High power for 1 minute.

3 Stir in the beets, bay leaf, thyme, lemon juice, and bouillon. Cover and cook on High power for 12 minutes, stirring halfway through. Set aside, uncovered, for 5 minutes.

4 Remove and discard the bay leaf. Strain the vegetables and reserve the liquid in a pitcher.

5 Place the vegetables with a little of the reserved liquid in a food processor or blender and process to a smooth and creamy purée. Alternatively, either mash the vegetable with a potato masher or press through a strainer.

6 Pour the vegetable purée into a clean bowl with the reserved liquid and mix well. Season with salt and pepper to taste. Cover and cook on High power for 4–5 minutes or until piping hot.

7 Serve the soup in warmed bowls. Swirl 1 tablespoon of sour cream into each serving and garnish with a few sprigs of fresh dill.

SERVES 4

1 onion, chopped
12 oz/350 g potatoes, diced
1 small cooking apple, peeled, cored, and grated
3 tbsp water
1 tsp cumin seeds
1 lb 2 oz/500 g cooked beets, peeled and diced
1 bay leaf
pinch of dried thyme
1 tsp lemon juice
2½ cups hot vegetable bouillon
4 tbsp sour cream
salt and pepper
fresh dill sprigs, to garnish

NUTRITION
Calories *120*; Sugars *11 g*; Protein *4 g*; Carbohydrate *22 g*; Fat *2 g*; Saturates *1 g*

 easy

20 mins

 30 mins

In this satisfying soup, the eggplants are first roasted with carrots and parsnips, giving a special flavor. The lemon-garlic seasoning adds a kick.

Eggplant Soup

SERVES 4

1 tbsp olive oil, plus extra for brushing
1½ lb/700 g eggplant, halved lengthwise
1 carrot, halved
1 small parsnip, halved
2 onions, chopped finely
3 garlic cloves, chopped finely
4 cups vegetable bouillon
¼ tsp fresh thyme leaves, or a pinch of dried thyme
1 bay leaf
⅛ tsp ground coriander
1 tbsp tomato paste
⅔ cup light cream
freshly squeezed lemon juice
salt and pepper

lemon-garlic seasoning
grated zest of ½ lemon
1 garlic clove, chopped finely
3 tbsp chopped fresh parsley

NUTRITION
Calories *130*; Sugars *9 g*; Protein *3 g*;
Carbohydrate *12 g*; Fat *8 g*; Saturates *3 g*

   moderate

   20 mins

   1 hr 15 mins

1 Oil a shallow roasting pan and add the eggplant, cut sides down, and the carrot and parsnip. Brush the vegetables with oil. Roast in a preheated oven at 400°F/200°C for 30 minutes, turning once.

2 When cool enough to handle, scrape the eggplant flesh away from the skin, or scoop it out, then roughly chop. Cut the parsnip and carrot into chunks.

3 Heat the oil in a large pan over medium-low heat. Add the onions and garlic and cook for about 5 minutes, stirring frequently, until soft. Add the eggplant, parsnip, carrot, bouillon, thyme, bay leaf, coriander, and tomato paste, with a little salt. Stir to combine. Cover and simmer for 30 minutes or until the vegetables are very tender.

4 Let the soup cool slightly, then transfer to a blender or food processor and purée until smooth, working in batches if necessary. (If using a food processor, strain off the cooking liquid and reserve. Purée the soup solids with enough cooking liquid to moisten them, then combine with the remaining liquid.)

5 Return the puréed soup to the pan and stir in the cream. Reheat the soup over low heat for about 10 minutes or until hot. Adjust the seasoning, adding lemon juice to taste.

6 To make the lemon-garlic seasoning, chop together the lemon zest, garlic, and parsley until very fine and well mixed. Ladle the soup into warmed bowls, then garnish with the lemon-garlic seasoning.

For the most robust flavor, use bacon that has been fairly heavily smoked and has a pronounced taste; for a more delicate soup, use unsmoked bacon.

Smoky Green Bean Soup

1 Heat the oil in a large wide pan over a medium heat. Add the bacon and cook for 8–10 minutes or until golden. Remove the bacon from the pan with a slotted spoon and drain on paper towels. Pour off all the fat from the pan.

2 Add the onion and garlic to the pan and cook for about 3 minutes, stirring frequently, until the onion begins to soften.

3 Stir in the flour and continue cooking for 2 minutes. Add half of the water and stir well, scraping the bottom of the pan to mix in the flour.

4 Add the leek, carrot, potato, beans, and bay leaf. Stir in the remaining water and season with salt and pepper. Bring just to a boil, stirring occasionally, reduce the heat and simmer, partially covered, for 35–40 minutes or until the beans are very tender.

5 Allow the soup to cool slightly, then transfer to a blender or food processor, and purée until smooth, working in batches if necessary. (If using a food processor, strain off the cooking liquid and reserve. Purée the soup solids with enough cooking liquid to moisten them, then combine with the remaining liquid.)

6 Return the soup to the pan, add the bacon, and simmer over a low heat for a few minutes or until heated through, stirring occasionally. Taste and adjust the seasoning, adding nutmeg, pepper and, if needed, more salt. Sprinkle with croûtons to serve.

SERVES 4

1 tbsp oil
3½ oz/100 g lean smoked back bacon, chopped finely
1 onion, finely chopped
1–2 garlic cloves, chopped finely or crushed
2 tbsp all-purpose flour
5 cups water
1 leek, sliced thinly
1 carrot, chopped finely
1 small potato, chopped finely
1 lb 2 oz/500 g green beans
1 bay leaf
freshly grated nutmeg
salt and pepper
garlic croûtons, to garnish (see page 89)

NUTRITION
Calories 192; Sugars 7 g; Protein 9 g; Carbohydrate 22 g; Fat 8 g; Saturates 2 g

 moderate

15 mins

1 hr

This fresh-tasting soup with green beans, cucumber, and watercress can be served warm, or chilled on a hot summer day.

Green Soup

SERVES 4

1 tbsp olive oil

1 onion, chopped

1 garlic clove, chopped

7 oz/200 g potato, cut into 1-inch/2.5-cm cubes

3 cups vegetable or chicken bouillon

1 small cucumber or ½ large cucumber, cut into chunks

3 oz/85 g watercress

4½ oz/125 g green beans, trimmed and halved lengthwise

salt and pepper

1 Heat the oil in a large pan and cook the onion and garlic over medium heat for 3–4 minutes or until softened.

2 Add the cubed potato and cook for a further 2–3 minutes. Stir in the bouillon and bring to a boil. Lower the heat and simmer for 5 minutes.

3 Add the cucumber to the pan and cook for a further 3 minutes or until the potatoes are tender. Test by inserting the tip of a knife into the potato cubes—it should pass through easily.

4 Add the watercress and cook until just wilted. Remove from heat and set aside to cool slightly, then transfer to a food processor, and process to a smooth purée. Alternatively, before adding the watercress, mash the vegetables with a potato masher and push through a strainer, then chop the watercress finely and stir into the soup.

5 Bring a small pan of water to a boil and steam the beans for 3–4 minutes or until tender. Add the beans to the soup, season to taste with salt and pepper, and warm through. Ladle into warmed soup bowls and serve immediately or set aside to cool and then chill.

NUTRITION

Calories *121*; Sugars *2 g*; Protein *2 g*; Carbohydrate *10 g*; Fat *8 g*; Saturates *1 g*

easy

15–45 mins

25 mins

🍳 **COOK'S TIP**

Try using 4½ oz/125 g snow peas instead of the beans. You can also use spinach if watercress is unavailable.

Adding soft cheese to this soup just before serving makes it very special, while the rice and croûtons provide an excellent contrast of textures.

Broccoli Soup

1 Divide the broccoli into small flowerets and cut off the stems. Peel the large stems and then chop all the stems into small pieces.

2 Heat the butter and oil in a large pan over medium heat and add the onion, leek, and carrot. Cook for 3–4 minutes, stirring frequently, until the onion is soft.

3 Add the broccoli stems, rice, water, bay leaf, and a pinch of salt. Bring just to a boil and reduce the heat to low. Cover and simmer for 15 minutes. Add the broccoli flowerets to the pan and continue cooking, covered, for 15–20 minutes or until the rice and vegetables are tender. Remove the bay leaf.

4 Stir in the cream and cream cheese. Season the soup with nutmeg, pepper, and, if needed, more salt. Simmer over low heat for a few minutes until heated through, stirring occasionally. Taste and adjust the seasoning, if needed.

5 Ladle into warmed bowls and serve garnished with croûtons.

SERVES 4

1 lb/450 g broccoli (from 1 large head)
2 tsp butter
1 tsp oil
1 onion, chopped finely
1 leek, sliced thinly
1 small carrot, chopped finely
3 tbsp white rice
3¾ cups water
1 bay leaf
4 tbsp heavy cream
½ cup cream cheese
freshly grated nutmeg
salt and pepper
croûtons, to garnish (see Cook's Tip)

 COOK'S TIP

To make croûtons, remove the crusts from thick slices of bread, then cut the bread into dice. Fry in vegetable oil, stirring constantly, until evenly browned, then drain on paper towels.

NUTRITION
Calories *384*; Sugars *7 g*; Protein *8 g*; Carbohydrate *21 g*; Fat *30 g*; Saturates *18 g*

 moderate

15 mins

40 mins

This soup has a rich brilliant color and an intense pure flavor. Ready-washed spinach makes it especially quick to make.

Spinach Soup

SERVES 4

1 tbsp olive oil
1 onion, halved and thinly sliced
1 leek, split lengthwise and sliced thinly
1 potato, diced finely
4 cups water
2 sprigs fresh marjoram or ¼ tsp dried marjoram
2 sprigs fresh thyme or ¼ tsp dried thyme
1 bay leaf
14 oz/400 g young spinach
freshly grated nutmeg
salt and pepper
4 tbsp light cream, to serve

NUTRITION

Calories *98*; Sugars *4 g*; Protein *4 g*;
Carbohydrate *12 g*; Fat *4 g*; Saturates *1 g*

  easy

  10 mins

  40 mins

1 Heat the oil in a heavy pan over medium heat. Add the onion and leek and cook, stirring occasionally, for about 3 minutes or until they are just beginning to soften.

2 Add the potato, water, marjoram, thyme, and bay leaf and season with a pinch of salt. Bring to a boil, reduce the heat, cover, and cook gently for about 25 minutes or until the vegetables are tender. Remove the bay leaf and the herb stems.

3 Add the spinach and continue cooking for 3–4 minutes, stirring frequently, just until it is completely wilted. Remove the pan from the heat and set aside to cool slightly.

4 Transfer the soup to a blender or food processor and process to a smooth smooth purée, working in batches if necessary. (If using a food processor, strain off the cooking liquid and reserve. Process the soup solids with enough cooking liquid to moisten them, then combine with the remaining liquid.)

5 Return the soup to the pan and thin with a little more water, if wished. Season to taste with salt, pepper, and nutmeg. Place over low heat and simmer until reheated. Ladle the soup into warmed bowls and swirl a tablespoonful of cream into each serving.

The exotic flavors give this simple soup a lift. If you wish, use store-bought ginger paste instead of grating it; add to taste as the strength varies.

Parsnip Soup *with* Ginger

1 Heat the olive oil in a large pan over medium heat. Add the onion and leek and cook, stirring occasionally, for about 5 minutes or until softened.

2 Add the parsnips, carrots, ginger, garlic, grated orange zest, water, and a pinch of salt. Reduce the heat, cover, and simmer, stirring occasionally, for about 40 minutes or until the vegetables have softened.

3 Remove from the heat and set aside to cool slightly, then transfer to a blender or food processor, and process to a smooth purée, in batches if necessary.

4 Return the soup to the pan and stir in the orange juice. Add a little water or more orange juice, if you prefer a thinner consistency. Taste and adjust the seasoning with salt and pepper.

5 Simmer for about 10 minutes to heat through. Ladle into warmed bowls, garnish with chives or slivers of scallion and serve immediately.

SERVES 4

2 tsp olive oil
1 large onion, chopped
1 large leek, sliced
1 lb 12 oz/800 g parsnips, sliced
2 carrots, sliced thinly
4 tbsp grated fresh gingerroot
2–3 garlic cloves, chopped finely
grated zest of ½ orange
6¼ cups water
1 cup orange juice
salt and pepper
chopped chives or slivers of scallion, to garnish

NUTRITION
Calories *151*; Sugars *19 g*; Protein *4 g*; Carbohydrate *29 g*; Fat *3 g*; Saturates *0 g*

    easy

10 mins

55 mins

COOK'S TIP

You could make the soup using equal amounts (1 lb/450 g each) of carrots and parsnips.

This soup has an intense, earthy flavor that brings to mind woodland aromas. It makes a memorable, rich-tasting appetizer.

Exotic Mushroom Soup

SERVES 4

1 oz/25 g dried porcini mushrooms
1½ cups boiling water
4½ oz/125 g fresh porcini mushrooms
2 tsp olive oil
1 celery stalk, chopped
1 carrot, chopped
1 onion, chopped
3 garlic cloves, crushed
5 cups vegetable bouillon or water
leaves from 2 fresh thyme sprigs
1 tbsp butter
3 tbsp dry or medium sherry
2–3 tbsp sour cream
salt and pepper
chopped fresh parsley, to garnish

NUTRITION
Calories *130*; Sugars *5 g*; Protein *3 g*;
Carbohydrate *6 g*; Fat *9 g*; Saturates *5 g*

 moderate

20 mins

1 hr

1 Soak the dried mushrooms in the boiling water for 10–15 minutes.

2 Brush or wash the fresh mushrooms. Trim and reserve the stems. Slice any large mushroom caps.

3 Heat the oil in a large pan over a medium heat. Add the celery, carrot, onion, and mushroom stems. Cook, stirring frequently, for about 8 minutes or until the onion browns. Stir in the garlic and cook for 1 minute.

4 Add the vegetable bouillon and thyme with a pinch of salt. Add the soaked dried mushrooms to the pan. Strain the soaking liquid through a cheesecloth-lined strainer into the pan. Bring to a boil, reduce the heat, partially cover, and simmer gently for 30–40 minutes or until the carrots are tender.

5 Remove the pan from the heat and set aside to cool slightly, then transfer the soup solids with enough of the cooking liquid to moisten to a blender or food processor, and process to a smooth purée. Return it to the pan, combine with the remaining cooking liquid, cover, and simmer gently.

6 Meanwhile, melt the butter in a skillet over medium heat. Add the fresh mushroom caps and season to taste with salt and pepper. Cook, stirring occasionally, for about 8 minutes or until they start to color. When the skillet becomes dry, add the sherry and cook briefly.

7 Add the mushrooms and sherry to the soup. Taste and adjust the seasoning, if necessary. Ladle into warmed soup bowls, put a spoon of sour cream in each and garnish with parsley and serve.

Include some pungent greens in this soup, if you can. They add a wonderful gutsy flavor and, of course, are very good for you.

Beans *and* Greens Soup

1 Cover the beans with cold water and soak for 6 hours or overnight. Drain, put in a pan and add water to cover by 2 inches/5 cm. Bring to a boil and boil for 10 minutes. Drain and rinse.

2 Heat the olive oil in a large pan over medium heat. Add the onion and cook, stirring occasionally, for about 3–4 minutes or until just softened. Add the garlic, celery, and carrots and continue cooking for 2 minutes.

3 Add the water, beans, thyme, marjoram, and bay leaf. When the mixture begins to simmer, reduce the heat to low. Cover and simmer gently, stirring occasionally, for about 1¼ hours or until the beans are tender. The cooking time will vary depending on the type of bean. Season to taste with salt and pepper.

4 Remove the pan from the heat and set aside to cool slightly, then transfer 2 cups to a blender or food processor. Process to a smooth purée and recombine with the soup.

5 Cut the greens crosswise into thin ribbons, keeping tender leaves, such as spinach, separate. Add the thicker leaves and cook gently for 10 minutes. Stir in any remaining greens and cook for a further 5–10 minutes or until all the greens are tender. Taste and adjust the seasoning if necessary. Ladle the soup into warmed bowls and serve immediately.

SERVES 4

1½ cups dried navy or cannellini beans
1 tbsp olive oil
2 onions, chopped finely
4 garlic cloves, chopped finely
1 celery stalk, sliced thinly
2 carrots, halved and thinly sliced
5 cups water
¼ tsp dried thyme
¼ tsp dried marjoram
1 bay leaf
4 oz/115 g leafy greens, such as Swiss chard, mustard, spinach, and kale, washed
salt and pepper

NUTRITION
Calories *282*; Sugars *8 g*; Protein *16 g*; Carbohydrate *46 g*; Fat *4 g*; Saturates *1 g*

 easy

6 hrs 15 mins

 2 hrs

This soup is surprisingly delicate. The yellow peas give it an appealing light color, while the parsnips add an aromatic flavor.

Split Pea *and* Parsnip Soup

SERVES 4

generous 1 cup split yellow peas
1 tbsp olive oil
1 onion, chopped finely
1 small leek, chopped finely
3 garlic cloves, chopped finely
2 parsnips, sliced (about 8 oz/225 g)
2 quarts water
10 fresh sage leaves or ¼ tsp dried sage
pinch of dried thyme
¼ tsp ground coriander
1 bay leaf
salt and pepper
freshly grated nutmeg
chopped fresh cilantro leaves or parsley,
    to garnish

NUTRITION
Calories 270; Sugars 5 g; Protein 16 g;
Carbohydrate 39 g; Fat 7 g; Saturates 1 g

easy

10 mins

1 hr

1 Rinse the peas well under cold running water. Put in a pan and cover generously with water. Bring to a boil and boil for 3 minutes, skimming off the foam from the surface. Drain the peas.

2 Heat the oil in a large pan over medium heat. Add the onion and leek and cook, stirring occasionally, for about 3 minutes or until just softened. Add the garlic and parsnips and continue cooking, stirring occasionally, for 2 minutes.

3 Add the peas, water, sage, thyme, coriander, and bay leaf. Bring almost to a boil, reduce the heat, cover, and simmer gently for about 40 minutes or until the vegetables are very soft. Remove the bay leaf.

4 Remove the pan from the heat and set aside to cool slightly, then transfer to a blender or food processor, and process to a smooth purée, in batches if necessary. (If using a food processor, strain off the cooking liquid and reserve. Purée the soup solids with enough cooking liquid to moisten them, then combine with the remaining liquid.)

5 Return the soup to the pan and thin with a little more water, if wished. Season generously with salt, pepper, and nutmeg. Place over low heat and simmer until reheated. Ladle into warmed soup plates and garnish with fresh cilantro leaves or parsley.

This is a hearty and flavorful soup that is good on its own or spooned over cooked rice or baked potatoes for a more substantial meal.

Vegetable Chili

1 Brush the eggplant slices on 1 side with olive oil. Heat half the oil in a large, heavy skillet over medium-high heat. Add the eggplant slices, oiled side up, and cook for 5–6 minutes or until browned. Turn the slices over, cook on the other side until browned and then transfer to a plate. Cut the slices into bite-size pieces.

2 Heat the remaining oil in a large pan over medium heat. Add the onion and bell peppers and cook, stirring occasionally, for 3–4 minutes or until the onion is just softened, but not browned. Add the garlic and continue cooking for 2–3 minutes or until the onion is just beginning to color.

3 Add the tomatoes, chili powder, cumin, and oregano. Season to taste with salt and pepper. Bring just to a boil, reduce the heat, cover, and simmer gently for 15 minutes.

4 Add the zucchini, eggplant pieces, and kidney beans. Stir in the water and tomato paste. Bring back to a boil, cover, and continue simmering for about 45 minutes or until the vegetables are tender. Taste and adjust the seasoning if necessary. If you prefer a hotter dish, stir in a little more chili powder.

5 Ladle into warmed bowls and top with scallions and cheese.

SERVES 4

1 medium eggplant, peeled if wished, cut into 1-inch/2.5-cm slices
1 tbsp olive oil, plus extra for brushing
1 large red or yellow onion, chopped finely
2 red or yellow bell peppers, seeded and finely chopped
3–4 garlic cloves, chopped finely or crushed
28 oz/800g canned chopped tomatoes
1 tbsp mild chili powder
½ tsp ground cumin
½ tsp dried oregano
2 small zucchini, quartered lengthwise and sliced
14 oz/400g canned kidney beans, drained and rinsed
2 cups water
1 tbsp tomato paste
6 scallions, finely chopped
1 cup grated Cheddar cheese
salt and pepper

NUTRITION
Calories 213; Sugars 11 g; Protein 12 g; Carbohydrate 21 g; Fat 10 g; Saturates 5 g

easy

10 mins

1 hr 15 mins

This soup is simple and satisfying, with subtle flavors. It uses ingredients you are likely to have at hand, so it's ideal for a last-minute meal.

Tomato *and* Lentil Soup

SERVES 6

1 tbsp olive oil
1 leek, thinly sliced
1 large carrot, quartered and thinly sliced
1 large onion, chopped finely
2 garlic cloves, chopped finely
generous 1 cup split red lentils
5 cups water
1½ cups tomato juice
14 oz/400 g canned chopped tomatoes
¼ tsp ground cumin
¼ tsp ground coriander
1 bay leaf
salt and pepper
chopped fresh dill or parsley, to garnish

NUTRITION
Calories *194*; Sugars *9 g*; Protein *12 g*;
Carbohydrate *33 g*; Fat *3 g*; Saturates *0 g*

easy

10 mins

1 hr

1 Heat the oil in a large pan over medium heat. Add the leek, carrot, onion, and garlic. Cover and cook, stirring occasionally, for 4–5 minutes or until the vegetables are slightly softened.

2 Rinse and drain the lentils (check for any small stones). Add the lentils to the pan and stir in the water, tomato juice, and tomatoes. Add the cumin, coriander, and bay leaf with a pinch of salt. Bring to a boil, reduce the heat, and simmer gently for about 45 minutes or until the vegetables are tender. Remove the bay leaf.

3 Remove the pan from the heat and set aside to cool slightly. If you prefer a smooth soup, transfer the mixture to a blender or food processor and process to a smooth purée, working in batches if necessary. (If using a food processor, strain off the cooking liquid and reserve. Purée the soup solids with enough cooking liquid to moisten them, then combine with the remaining liquid.) Process only about half of the mixture if you prefer a soup with a chunkier texture.

4 Return the puréed soup to the pan and stir to blend. Season with salt and pepper to taste. Simmer over medium-low heat until reheated.

5 Ladle the soup into warmed bowls, garnish with dill or parsley, and serve.

This soup is a typical Indian treatment of lentils, called dhal. Often dhals are served as a thick purée, but in this version the consistency is slightly thinner to make it easier for spooning.

Curried Lentil Soup *with* Fried Onions

1 Heat the olive oil in a large pan over a medium heat. Add the onion and cook for 4–5 minutes, stirring frequently, until it just begins to brown. Add the leek, carrot, and garlic and cook for 2 minutes, stirring occasionally.

2 Stir in the chili paste, ginger, garam masala or curry powder, cumin, and turmeric. Add the water and stir to mix well.

3 Rinse and drain the lentils (check for any small stones). Add to the pan. Bring to a boil, reduce the heat, cover, and simmer gently for 35 minutes or until the lentils and vegetables are very soft, stirring occasionally.

4 Allow the soup to cool slightly, then transfer to a blender or food processor and purée until smooth, working in batches if necessary. (If using a food processor, strain off the cooking liquid and reserve. Purée the soup solids with enough cooking liquid to moisten them, then combine with the remaining liquid.)

5 Return the soup to the pan and simmer over a low heat. Season with salt and pepper to taste.

6 For the fried onions, heat about ½ inch/1 cm oil in a small skillet over a medium-high heat until it begins to smoke. Drop in about one-third of the onion slices and fry until deep golden brown. Using a slotted spoon, transfer to paper towels. Cook the remainder of the onion slices in batches and drain.

7 Ladle the soup into warmed bowls and scatter the fried onions over the top. Serve the soup immediately.

SERVES 4

2 tsp olive oil
1 large onion, chopped finely
1 large leek, sliced thinly
1 large carrot, grated
1–2 garlic cloves, chopped finely
½ tsp chili paste
½ tsp grated peeled fresh gingerroot or ginger paste
½ tsp garam masala or curry powder
¼ tsp ground cumin
⅛ tsp ground turmeric
5 cups water
generous 1 cup split red lentils or yellow split peas
salt and pepper

to garnish
1 red onion, halved and thinly sliced into half-rings
oil, for frying

NUTRITION
Calories *232*; Sugars *6 g*; Protein *11 g*; Carbohydrate *31 g*; Fat *8 g*; Saturates *1 g*

 moderate

10 mins

55 mins

In this simple-to-make soup, the flavors meld together after blending to create a delicious taste. It is also very healthy and looks appealing.

Golden Vegetable Soup

SERVES 6

1 tbsp olive oil
1 onion, chopped finely
1 garlic clove, chopped finely
1 carrot, halved and thinly sliced
1 lb/450 g green cabbage, shredded
14 oz/400 g canned chopped tomatoes
½ tsp dried thyme
2 bay leaves
6¾ cups vegetable bouillon
scant 1 cup Puy lentils
2 cups water
salt and pepper
fresh cilantro leaves or parsley, to garnish

1 Heat the oil in a large pan over medium heat. Add the onion, garlic, and carrot and cook, stirring occasionally, for 3–4 minutes. Add the cabbage and cook for a further 2 minutes.

2 Add the tomatoes, thyme, and 1 bay leaf, then pour in the bouillon. Bring to a boil, reduce the heat, partially cover, and simmer for about 45 minutes or until the vegetables are tender.

3 Meanwhile, put the lentils in another pan with the remaining bay leaf and the water. Bring just to a boil, reduce the heat, and simmer for about 25 minutes or until tender. Drain off any remaining water and set aside.

4 Remove the soup pan from the heat and set aside to cool slightly, then transfer to a blender or food processor, and process to a smooth purée, working in batches, if necessary. (If using a food processor, strain off the cooking liquid and reserve. Purée the soup solids with enough cooking liquid to moisten them, then combine with the remaining liquid.)

5 Return the soup to the pan and add the cooked lentils. Taste and adjust the seasoning, if necessary, and cook for about 10 minutes to heat through. Ladle into warmed bowls and garnish with coriander leaves or parsley.

NUTRITION
Calories 155; Sugars 5 g; Protein 10 g;
Carbohydrate 22 g; Fat 3 g; Saturates 0 g

 easy

 10 mins

1 hr 10 mins

This rustic vegetable soup is appealing in its simplicity. Served with ciabatta, focaccia, or garlic bread, it makes a good light lunch.

Fennel *and* Broccoli Soup

1 Rinse the barley and drain. Bring 2 cups of the bouillon to a boil in a small pan. Add the bay leaf and thyme. Add a pinch of salt. Stir in the barley, reduce the heat, partially cover, and simmer for about 30–40 minutes or until tender.

2 Cut the broccoli into flowerets and peel the stems. Cut the stems into very thin batons, about 1 inch/2.5 cm long. Cut the flowerets into small slivers and reserve them separately.

3 Heat the oil in a large pan over medium-low heat and add the leek and garlic. Cook, stirring frequently, for about 5 minutes or until softened. Add the celery, fennel, and broccoli stems and cook for 2 minutes.

4 Stir in the remaining bouillon and bring to a boil. Add the barley with its cooking liquid. Season to taste with salt and pepper. Reduce the heat, cover the pan, and simmer gently, stirring occasionally, for 10 minutes.

5 Uncover the pan and adjust the heat so the soup bubbles gently. Stir in the broccoli flowerets and cook for a further 10–12 minutes or until the broccoli is tender. Stir in the basil. Taste and adjust the seasoning if necessary. Ladle into warmed bowls and serve with plenty of Parmesan cheese to sprinkle over.

SERVES 4

1/4 cup pearl barley
6 1/4 cups chicken or vegetable bouillon
1 bay leaf
1/2 tsp chopped fresh thyme leaves, or 1/8 tsp dried thyme
9 oz/250 g broccoli
2 tsp olive oil
1 large leek, halved lengthwise and chopped finely
2 garlic cloves, chopped finely
1 celery stalk, sliced thinly
1 large fennel bulb, sliced thinly
1 tbsp chopped fresh basil
salt and pepper
freshly grated Parmesan cheese, to serve

NUTRITION
Calories *108*; Sugars *3 g*; Protein *6 g*; Carbohydrate *15 g*; Fat *3 g*; Saturates *0 g*

 moderate

15 mins

1 hr 15 mins

Although it is generally classed as a grain, wild rice is actually a native North American grass that grows in water. It adds a delicious texture to this soup.

Wild Rice *and* Spinach Soup

SERVES 4

2 tsp olive oil

3 oz/80 g smoked Canadian bacon, chopped finely

1 large onion, chopped finely

⅔ cup wild rice, rinsed in cold water and drained

5 cups water

1–2 garlic cloves, chopped finely or crushed

1 bay leaf

½ cup all-purpose flour

2 cups milk

225 g/8 oz spinach leaves, chopped finely

1 cup heavy cream

freshly grated nutmeg

salt and pepper

croûtons, to garnish (see page 25)

NUTRITION
Calories *602*; Sugars *12 g*; Protein *14 g*; Carbohydrate *51 g*; Fat *39 g*; Saturates *20 g*

easy

15 mins

1 hr 15 mins

1 Heat the oil in a large pan over a medium heat. Add the smoked Canadian bacon and cook for 6–7 minutes or until lightly browned. Add the onion and wild rice and continue cooking for 3–4 minutes, stirring frequently, until the onion softens.

2 Add the water, garlic, and bay leaf and season with a little salt and pepper. Bring to a boil, reduce the heat, cover, and boil very gently for about 1 hour or until some of the grains of wild rice have split open.

3 Put the flour in a mixing bowl and very slowly whisk in enough of the milk to make a thick paste. Add the remainder of the milk, whisking to make a smooth liquid. Put the flour and milk mixture in a pan and ladle in as much of the rice cooking liquid as possible. Bring to a boil, stirring almost constantly. Reduce the heat so that the liquid just bubbles gently and cook for 10 minutes, stirring occasionally. Add the spinach and cook for 1–2 minutes or until wilted.

4 Allow the soup to cool slightly, then transfer to a blender or food processor and purée, working in batches if necessary. (If using a food processor, strain off the cooking liquid and reserve. Purée the soup solids with enough cooking liquid to moisten them, then combine with the remaining liquid.)

5 Combine the puréed soup with the rice mixture in a pan and place over a medium-low heat. Stir in the cream and a grating of nutmeg. Simmer the soup until reheated. Taste and adjust the seasoning, if needed, ladle into warmed bowls, and garnish with croutons.

This healthy and colorful soup makes good use of your herb garden. The fresh herbs give it a vibrant flavor.

Vegetable Soup *with* Bulgur

1 Heat the oil in a large pan over medium-low heat and add the onions and garlic. Cook for 5–8 minutes, stirring occasionally, until the onions soften.

2 Stir in the bulgur and continue cooking, stirring constantly, for 1 minute.

3 Layer the tomatoes, pumpkin or squash, and zucchini in the pan.

4 Combine half the water with the tomato paste, chili paste, and a pinch of salt. Pour over the vegetables. Cover and simmer for 15 minutes.

5 Uncover the pan and stir. Put all the herbs and the arugula on top of the soup and layer the peas over them. Pour in the remaining water and gradually bring to a boil. Reduce the heat and simmer for about 20–25 minutes or until all the vegetables are tender.

6 Stir the soup. Taste and adjust the seasoning, adding salt and pepper, if necessary, and a little more chili paste if you wish. Ladle into warmed bowls and serve with Parmesan cheese.

SERVES 4

1 tbsp olive oil

2 onions, chopped

3 garlic cloves, chopped finely or crushed

1/3 cup bulgur

5 tomatoes, peeled and sliced or 14 oz/400 g canned plum tomatoes in juice

1³/4 cups peeled diced pumpkin or acorn squash

1 large zucchini, quartered lengthwise and sliced

4 cups boiling water

2 tbsp tomato paste

1/4 tsp chili paste

1¹/2 oz/40 g chopped mixed fresh oregano, basil, and flat leaf parsley

1 oz/25 g arugula leaves, chopped coarsely

1¹/2 cups shelled fresh or frozen peas

salt and pepper

freshly grated Parmesan cheese, to serve

NUTRITION
Calories *93*; Sugars *8 g*; Protein *5 g*; Carbohydrate *13 g*; Fat *3 g*; Saturates *0 g*

 easy

 10 mins

1 hr

Hot *and* Spicy

Soups are a part of nearly every meal in the Far East, and are usually served between courses to clear the palate. This chapter provides a range of soups from all over the East, from thick Indian dhal soups to hot, sour Chinese vegetarian soups and combinations of seafood and noodles. All the ingredients are readily available from good stores, and although several recipes demand a little time, all are worth any extra effort in the making.

Parsnips make a delicious soup as they have a slightly sweet flavor. In this recipe, spices are added to complement this sweetness.

Curried Parsnip Soup

SERVES 4

1 tbsp vegetable oil
1 tbsp butter
1 red onion, chopped
3 parsnips, chopped
2 garlic cloves, crushed
2 tsp garam masala
½ tsp chili powder
1 tbsp all-purpose flour
3½ cups vegetable bouillon
grated zest and juice of 1 lemon
salt and pepper
lemon zest, to garnish

1 Heat the vegetable oil and butter in a large pan until the butter has melted. Add the onion, parsnips, and garlic and cook, stirring frequently, for about 5–7 minutes or until the vegetables are soft, but not colored.

2 Add the garam masala and chili powder and cook, stirring constantly, for 30 seconds. Sprinkle in the flour, mixing well, and cook, stirring constantly, for a further 30 seconds.

3 Stir in the bouillon, lemon zest, and lemon juice and bring to a boil. Reduce the heat and simmer for 20 minutes.

4 Remove some of the vegetable pieces with a slotted spoon and reserve until required. Transfer the remaining soup and vegetables to a food processor or blender and process for about 1 minute or until a smooth purée is formed. Alternatively, press the vegetables through a strainer with the back of a wooden spoon.

5 Return the soup to a clean pan and stir in the reserved vegetables. Heat the soup through for 2 minutes or until piping hot.

6 Season to taste with salt and pepper, then transfer to soup bowls, garnish with lemon zest, and serve.

NUTRITION
Calories *152*; Sugars *7 g*; Protein *3 g*;
Carbohydrate *18 g*; Fat *8 g*; Saturates *3 g*

 very easy

10 mins

35 mins

This soup can be frozen, so it is a good way to use up a glut of zucchini. Adding curry powder gives the flavor a lift.

Curried Zucchini Soup

1 Melt the butter in a large pan over medium heat. Add the onion and cook for about 3 minutes or until it begins to soften.

2 Add the bouillon, zucchini, and curry powder, along with a large pinch of salt if using unsalted bouillon. Bring the soup to a boil, reduce the heat, cover, and cook gently for about 25 minutes or until the vegetables are tender.

3 Let the soup cool slightly, then transfer to a blender or food processor, working in batches if necessary. Purée the soup until just smooth, but still with green flecks. (If using a food processor, strain off the cooking liquid and reserve. Purée the soup solids with enough cooking liquid to moisten them, then combine with the remaining liquid.)

4 Return the soup to the pan and stir in the sour cream. Reheat gently over low heat until the soup is just hot, but do not let it boil.

5 Taste the soup, adjust the seasoning, if necessary, ladle into warmed bowls, and serve immediately. If liked, garnish with a swirl of sour cream, a little curry powder, and some croûtons.

SERVES 4

2 tsp butter
1 large onion, chopped finely
2 lb/900 g zucchini, sliced
2 cups vegetable bouillon
1 tsp curry powder
½ cup sour cream
salt and pepper

to garnish
sour cream, optional
curry powder, optional
croûtons, optional

NUTRITION
Calories *147*; Sugars *8 g*; Protein *6 g*;
Carbohydrate *10 g*; Fat *9 g*; Saturates *5 g*

  moderate

10 mins

35 mins

🍳 **COOK'S TIP**

Bouillon made from a cube or liquid bouillon base is fine for this soup. In this case, you may wish to add a little more sour cream. The soup freezes well, but freeze it without the cream and add before serving.

Dhal is a delicious Indian lentil dish. This soup is a variation on the theme, made with red lentils and spiced with curry powder.

Dhal Soup

SERVES 4

2 tbsp butter
2 garlic cloves, chopped finely
1 onion, chopped
½ tsp turmeric
1 tsp garam masala
¼ tsp chili powder
1 tsp ground cumin
2 lb/900 g canned chopped tomatoes, drained
1 cup red lentils
2 tsp lemon juice
2½ cups vegetable bouillon
1¼ cups coconut milk
salt and pepper
chopped cilantro and lemon slices, to garnish
nan bread, to serve

1 Melt the butter in a large pan and cook the garlic and onion for 2–3 minutes, stirring. Add the spices and cook for a further 30 seconds.

2 Stir in the tomatoes, red lentils, lemon juice, vegetable bouillon, and coconut milk, and bring to a boil.

3 Reduce the heat and simmer for 25–30 minutes or until the lentils are tender and cooked.

4 Season to taste and spoon the soup into a warmed tureen. Garnish with chopped cilantro and lemon slices and serve with warm nan bread.

NUTRITION
Calories 284; Sugars 13 g; Protein 16 g; Carbohydrate 38 g; Fat 9 g; Saturates 5 g

 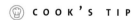

easy

5 mins

40 mins

COOK'S TIP

You can buy cans of coconut milk from stores and supermarkets. It can also be made by grating creamed coconut, which comes in the form of a solid bar, and mixing it with water.

Avocado has a rich flavor and color which makes a creamy flavored soup. It is best served chilled, but may be eaten warm as well.

Avocado *and* Vegetable Soup

1 Peel the avocado and mash the flesh with a fork, stir in the lemon juice, and reserve until required.

2 Heat the vegetable oil in a large pan. Add the corn, tomatoes, garlic, leek, and chile and cook over low heat for 2–3 minutes or until the vegetables are soft.

3 Put half the vegetable mixture in a food processor or blender, together with the mashed avocado, and process until smooth. Transfer the mixture to a clean pan.

4 Add the vegetable bouillon, milk, and reserved vegetables and cook over low heat for 3–4 minutes or until hot.

5 Transfer to warmed individual serving bowls, garnish with shredded leek, and serve immediately.

SERVES 4

1 large, ripe avocado
2 tbsp lemon juice
1 tbsp vegetable oil
2 tbsp canned corn kernels, drained
2 tomatoes, peeled and seeded
1 garlic clove, crushed
1 leek, chopped
1 fresh red chile, chopped
1¾ cups vegetable bouillon
⅔ cup milk
shredded leek, to garnish

NUTRITION
Calories *167*; Sugars *5 g*; Protein *4 g*; Carbohydrate *8 g*; Fat *13 g*; Saturates *3 g*

 very easy
15 mins
10 mins

 COOK'S TIP

If serving chilled, transfer from the food processor to a bowl, stir in the vegetable bouillon and milk, cover, and chill in the refrigerator for at least 4 hours.

This is a very colorful and delicious soup. If spinach is not in season, use lettuce or watercress instead.

Spinach *and* Bean Curd Soup

SERVES 4

1 block firm bean curd
4¹⁄₂ oz/125 g spinach leaves without stems
3 cups Chinese Bouillon (see page 15) or water
1 tbsp light soy sauce
salt and pepper

1 Using a sharp knife, cut the bean curd into about ¹⁄₄-inch/5-mm pieces.

2 Wash the spinach leaves under cold, running water and drain well.

3 Cut the spinach leaves into small pieces or shreds, discarding any discolored leaves and tough stalks. (If possible, use fresh young spinach leaves, which have not yet developed tough ribs. Otherwise, it is important to cut out all the ribs and stems for this soup.) Set the spinach aside until required.

4 In a preheated wok or large skillet, bring the Chinese bouillon or water to a boil.

5 Add the bean curd cubes and light soy sauce, bring back to a boil, and simmer gently for about 2 minutes over medium heat.

6 Add the spinach and simmer for 1 more minute, stirring gently. Skim the surface of the soup to make it clear, and season to taste.

7 Transfer the soup into either a warmed soup tureen or warmed individual serving bowls. Serve with chopsticks to pick up the spinach and chunks of bean curd, and a broad, shallow spoon for drinking the soup.

NUTRITION

Calories *33*; Sugars *1 g*; Protein *4 g*; Carbohydrate *1 g*; Fat *2 g*; Saturates *0.2 g*

★ very easy

◔ 15 mins

◷ 10 mins

 COOK'S TIP

Soup is an integral part of a Chinese meal; it is usually presented in a large bowl in the center of the table, and consumed as the meal progresses. It serves as a refresher between dishes and as a beverage throughout the meal.

This healthy soup is made with an unusual combination of fruits and vegetables, creating a tantalizing flavor that will keep people guessing.

Sweet *and* Sour Cabbage Soup

1 Put the raisins in a bowl, pour over the orange juice, and soak for 15 minutes.

2 Heat the oil in a large pan over medium heat. Add the onion and cook, stirring occasionally, for 3–4 minutes or until it starts to soften. Add the cabbage and cook for a further 2 minutes, but do not let it brown.

3 Add the apples and apple juice, cover, and cook for 5 minutes. Stir in the tomatoes, tomato or vegetable juice, pineapple, and water. Season to taste with salt and pepper and add the vinegar. Add the golden raisins with the orange juice. Bring to a boil, reduce the heat, partially cover, and simmer for 1 hour or until the fruit and vegetables are tender.

4 Remove the pan from the heat and set aside to cool slightly. Transfer the soup to a blender or food processor and process to a smooth purée, working in batches if necessary. (If using a food processor, strain off the cooking liquid and reserve. Purée the soup solids with enough cooking liquid to moisten them, then combine with the remaining liquid.)

5 Return the soup to the pan and simmer gently for about 10 minutes to reheat. Ladle into warmed bowls. Garnish with mint leaves.

SERVES 4

½ cup golden raisins
½ cup orange juice
1 tbsp olive oil
1 large onion, chopped
9 oz/250 g cabbage, shredded
2 apples, peeled and diced
½ cup apple juice
14 oz/400 g canned peeled tomatoes
1 cup tomato or vegetable juice
3½ oz/100 g pineapple flesh, chopped finely
5 cups water
2 tsp wine vinegar
salt and pepper
fresh mint leaves, to garnish

NUTRITION
Calories *103*; Sugars *24 g*; Protein *2 g*; Carbohydrate *25 g*; Fat *0 g*; Saturates *0 g*

easy

25 mins

1 hr 30 mins

COOK'S TIP

You can use green or white cabbage to make this soup, but red cabbage would require a much longer cooking time. Savoy cabbage has too powerful a flavor.

This soup has a real Mediterranean flavor, using sweet red bell peppers, tomato, chili, and basil. It is great served with a warm olive bread.

Red Bell Pepper Soup

SERVES 4

8 oz/225 g red bell peppers, seeded and sliced
1 onion, sliced
2 garlic cloves, crushed
1 fresh green chile, chopped
1¼ cups strained tomatoes
2½ cups vegetable bouillon
2 tbsp chopped fresh basil
fresh basil sprigs, to garnish

1 Put the red bell peppers in a large, heavy pan with the onion, garlic, and chile. Add the strained tomatoes and vegetable bouillon and bring to a boil over medium heat, stirring constantly.

2 Reduce the heat to low and simmer for 20 minutes or until the bell peppers have softened. Drain, reserving the liquid and vegetables separately.

3 Purée the vegetables by pressing through a strainer with the back of a spoon. Alternatively, process in a food processor to a smooth purée.

4 Return the vegetable purée to a clean pan and add the reserved cooking liquid. Add the basil and heat through until hot. Garnish the soup with fresh basil sprigs and serve.

NUTRITION

Calories 55; Sugars 10 g; Protein 2 g;
Carbohydrate 11 g; Fat 0.5 g; Saturates 0.1 g

 very easy

5 mins

25 mins

🍴 **COOK'S TIP**

This soup is also delicious served cold with ⅔ cup plain yogurt swirled into it.

This delicious soup is a wonderful blend of colors and flavors. It is very hot, so if you prefer a milder taste, omit the seeds from the chiles.

Chili *and* Watercress Soup

1 Put all the ingredients for the bouillon into a pan and bring to a boil.

2 Simmer the bouillon for 5 minutes. Remove from the heat and strain, reserving the bouillon.

3 Heat the sunflower oil in a wok or large, heavy skillet and cook the bean curd over high heat for about 2 minutes, stirring constantly so that the bean curd cooks evenly on both sides. Add the strained bouillon to the skillet.

4 Add the mushrooms and cilantro and boil for 3 minutes.

5 Add the watercress and boil for a further 1 minute.

6 Serve immediately, garnished with red chile slices.

SERVES 4

1 tbsp sunflower oil
9 oz/250 g smoked bean curd, sliced
3 oz/90 g shiitake mushrooms, sliced
2 tbsp chopped fresh cilantro
1 large bunch watercress
1 fresh red chile, sliced finely, to garnish

bouillon

1 tbsp tamarind pulp
2 dried red chilies, chopped
2 kaffir lime leaves, torn in half
1-inch/2.5-cm piece gingerroot, chopped
2-inch/5-cm piece galangal, chopped
1 stalk lemon grass, chopped
1 onion, quartered
4 cups cold water

NUTRITION
Calories *90*; Sugars *1 g*; Protein *7 g*;
Carbohydrate *2 g*; Fat *6 g*; Saturates *1 g*

 moderate

 10 mins

 15 mins

 COOK'S TIP

You might like to try a mixture of different types of mushroom. Oyster, white, and straw mushrooms are all suitable.

Chinese mushrooms add an intense flavor to this soup. If they are unavailable, use open-cap mushrooms instead.

Chili Fish Soup

SERVES 4

½ oz/15 g dried Chinese mushrooms

2 tbsp sunflower oil

1 onion, sliced

1½ cups snow peas

3½ oz/100 g canned bamboo shoots, drained

3 tbsp sweet chili sauce

5 cups fish or vegetable bouillon

3 tbsp light soy sauce

2 tbsp fresh cilantro, plus extra to garnish (optional)

1 lb/450 g cod fillet, skinned and cubed

1 Place the mushrooms in a large bowl. Pour enough boiling water over to cover and let stand for 5 minutes. Drain the mushrooms thoroughly in a strainer. Using a sharp knife, roughly chop the mushrooms.

2 Heat the sunflower oil in a preheated wok or large, heavy-based pan. Add the onion to the wok and cook for 5 minutes or until softened.

3 Add the snow peas, bamboo shoots, chili sauce, bouillon, and soy sauce to the wok and bring to a boil.

4 Reduce the heat, add the cilantro and cod, and let simmer for 5 minutes or until the fish is cooked through.

5 Transfer to a warmed soup tureen or individual warmed serving bowls, garnish with extra cilantro, if liked, and serve hot.

NUTRITION

Calories *166*; Sugars *1 g*; Protein *23 g*; Carbohydrate *4 g*; Fat *7 g*; Saturates *1 g*

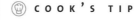

easy

15 mins

15 mins

 COOK'S TIP

There are many different varieties of dried mushrooms, but shiitake are best in this recipe. They are not cheap, but a small amount will go a long way.

This is a deliciously different fish soup which can be made quickly and easily in a microwave.

Asian Fish Soup

1 Beat the egg with the sesame seeds and seasoning. Lightly oil a plate and pour on the egg mixture. Cook in the microwave on High power for 1½ minutes or until just setting in the center. Leave to stand for a few minutes then remove from the plate. Roll up the egg and shred thinly.

2 Mix together the celery, carrot, scallions, and oil. Cover and cook on High power for 3 minutes.

3 Wash the spinach thoroughly under cold, running water. Cut off and discard any long stalks and drain well. Shred the spinach finely.

4 Add the hot bouillon, soy sauce, haddock, and spinach to the vegetable mixture. Cover and cook on High power for 5 minutes. Stir the soup and season to taste. Serve in warmed bowls, scattered with the shredded egg.

SERVES 4

1 egg
1 tsp sesame seeds, toasted
1 celery stalk, chopped
1 carrot, cut into julienne strips
4 scallions, sliced on the diagonal
1 tbsp oil
1½ cups fresh spinach
3½ cups hot vegetable bouillon
4 tsp light soy sauce
9 oz/250 g haddock, skinned and cut into small chunks
salt and pepper

NUTRITION
Calories *105*; Sugars *1 g*; Protein *13 g*; Carbohydrate *1 g*; Fat *5 g*; Saturates *1 g*

easy

20 mins

10 mins

 COOK'S TIP

Instead of topping the soup with omelet shreds, you could pour the beaten egg, without the sesame seeds, into the hot bouillon at the end of the cooking time. The egg will set in pretty strands to give a flowery look.

This soup is topped with small wontons filled with shrimp, making it both very tasty and satisfying.

Fish Soup *with* Wontons

SERVES 4

4½ oz/125 g large, cooked, peeled shrimp
1 tsp chopped chives
1 small garlic clove, chopped finely
1 tbsp vegetable oil
12 wonton wrappers
1 small egg, beaten
3¾ cups fish bouillon
6 oz/175 g white fish fillet, diced
dash of chili sauce
sliced fresh red chile and chives, to garnish

1 Roughly chop a quarter of the shrimp and mix together with the chopped chives and garlic.

2 Heat the oil in a preheated wok or large skillet until it is really hot.

3 Stir-fry the shrimp mixture for 1–2 minutes. Remove from the heat and set aside to cool completely.

4 Spread out the wonton wrappers on a counter. Spoon a little of the shrimp filling into the center of each wrapper. Brush the edges of the wrappers with beaten egg and press the edges together, scrunching them to form a "moneybag" shape. Set aside while you are preparing the soup.

5 Pour the fish bouillon into a large pan and bring to a boil. Add the diced white fish and the remaining shrimp and cook for 5 minutes.

6 Season to taste with the chili sauce. Add the wontons and cook for a further 5 minutes.

7 Spoon into warmed serving bowls, garnish with sliced red chile and chives and serve immediately.

NUTRITION
Calories 115; Sugars 0 g; Protein 16 g; Carbohydrate 1 g; Fat 5 g; Saturates 1 g

 moderate

10 mins

15 mins

 **COOK'S TIP**

Replace the shrimp with cooked crabmeat for an alternative flavor.

Ideally, use raw shrimp in this soup. If that is not possible, add ready-cooked ones at the very last stage.

Three-Flavor Soup

1 Using a sharp knife or meat cleaver, thinly slice the chicken into small shreds. If the shrimp are large, cut each in half lengthways, otherwise leave them whole.

2 Place the chicken and shrimp in a bowl and mix with a pinch of salt, the egg white, and cornstarch paste until well coated. Set aside until required.

3 Cut the honey-roast ham into small thin slices roughly the same size as the chicken pieces.

4 In a preheated wok or large, heavy skillet, bring the Chinese bouillon or water to a rolling boil and add the chicken, the raw shrimp, and the ham.

5 Bring the soup back to a boil, and simmer for 1 minute.

6 Adjust the seasoning to taste, then pour the soup into four warmed individual serving bowls, garnish with the scallions, and serve immediately.

SERVES 4

$4\frac{1}{2}$ oz/125 g skinned, boned chicken breast
$4\frac{1}{2}$ oz/125 g raw peeled shrimp
salt
$\frac{1}{2}$ egg white, lightly beaten
2 tsp cornstarch paste (see page 15)
$4\frac{1}{2}$ oz/125 g honey-roast ham
3 cups Chinese Bouillon (see page 15)
  or water
finely chopped scallions, to garnish

NUTRITION
Calories 117; Sugars 0 g; Protein 20 g;
Carbohydrate 2 g; Fat 3 g; Saturates 1 g

    easy
    3 hrs 30 mins
        10 mins

 COOK'S TIP

Soups such as this are improved enormously in flavor if you use a well-flavored bouillon. Either use a bouillon cube, or find time to make Chinese Bouillon (see page 15.) Better still, make double quantities and freeze some.

As taste and tolerance for chiles varies, using chili purée, instead of fresh chiles, offers more control of the heat.

Thai-Style Seafood Soup

SERVES 4

5 cups fish bouillon
1 lemongrass stalk, split lengthwise
pared zest of ½ lime or 1 lime leaf
1-inch/2.5-cm piece of fresh gingerroot, sliced
¼ tsp chili paste
4–6 scallions
7 oz/200 g large or medium raw shrimp, peeled and deveined
9 oz/250 g scallops (about 16–20)
2 tbsp fresh cilantro leaves
salt
finely chopped red bell pepper or fresh red chile rings, to garnish

1 Put the bouillon in a pan with the lemongrass, lime zest or lime leaf, ginger, and chili paste. Bring just to a boil, reduce the heat, cover, and simmer for 10–15 minutes.

2 Cut the scallions in half lengthwise, then slice crosswise very thinly. Cut the shrimp almost in half lengthwise, keeping the tails intact.

3 Strain the bouillon, return to the pan, and bring to a simmer, with bubbles rising at the edges and the surface trembling. Add the scallions and cook for 2–3 minutes. Taste and season with salt, if needed, and stir in a little more chili paste if wished.

4 Add the scallops and shrimp and poach for about 1 minute or until they turn opaque and the shrimp curl.

5 Add the cilantro leaves, ladle the soup into warmed bowls, and garnish with red bell pepper or chiles.

NUTRITION
Calories *132*; Sugars *7 g*; Protein *20 g*; Carbohydrate *9 g*; Fat *2 g*; Saturates *0 g*

 moderate

 10 mins

20 mins

 COOK'S TIP

Substitute very small baby leeks, slivered or thinly sliced diagonally, for the scallions. Include the green parts.

Use shrimp, squid, or scallops, or possibly a combination of all three in this healthy soup.

Seafood *and* Bean Curd Soup

1 Small shrimp can be left whole; larger ones should be cut into smaller pieces; cut the squid and scallops into small pieces.

2 If raw, mix the shrimp and scallops with the egg white and cornstarch paste to prevent them from becoming tough when they are cooked. Cut the cake of bean curd into about 24 small cubes.

3 Bring the bouillon to a rolling boil. Add the bean curd and soy sauce, bring back to a boil, and simmer for 1 minute.

4 Stir in the seafood, raw pieces first, pre-cooked ones last. Bring back to a boil and simmer for just 1 minute.

5 Adjust the seasoning to taste and serve, garnished with cilantro leaves, if liked.

SERVES 4

9 oz/250 g seafood: peeled shrimp, squid, scallops, etc., defrosted if frozen
½ egg white, lightly beaten
1 tbsp Cornstarch Paste (see page 15)
1 cake bean curd
3 cups Chinese Bouillon (see page 15)
1 tbsp light soy sauce
salt and pepper
fresh cilantro leaves, to garnish (optional)

NUTRITION
Calories *97*; Sugars *0 g*; Protein *17 g*; Carbohydrate *3 g*; Fat *2 g*; Saturates *0.4 g*

 moderate

 10 mins

10 mins

🍳 **COOK'S TIP**

Bean curd, also known as tofu, is made from puréed yellow soya beans, which are very high in protein. Almost tasteless, bean curd absorbs the flavors of other ingredients. It is widely available in supermarkets and health-food stores.

Aromatic lime leaves are used as a flavoring in this soup to add tartness.

Spicy Shrimp Soup

SERVES 4

2 tbsp tamarind paste
4 fresh red chiles, chopped very finely
2 garlic cloves, crushed
2 tsp finely chopped fresh gingerroot
4 tbsp fish sauce
2 tbsp palm sugar or superfine sugar
5 cups fish bouillon
8 lime leaves, roughly torn
3½ oz/100 g carrots, sliced thinly
12 oz/350 g sweet potato, diced
3½ oz/100 g baby corn cobs, halved
3 tbsp roughly chopped fresh cilantro
3½ oz/100 g cherry tomatoes, halved
8 oz/225 g raw shrimp

1 Place the tamarind paste, red chiles, garlic, ginger, fish sauce, palm or superfine sugar, and fish bouillon in a preheated wok or large, heavy-based pan. Add the lime leaves to the wok. Bring to a boil, stirring constantly, to blend the flavors.

2 Reduce the heat and add the carrot, sweet potato, and baby corn cobs to the mixture in the wok.

3 Leave the soup to simmer, uncovered, for about 10 minutes or until the vegetables are just tender.

4 Stir the cilantro, cherry tomatoes, and shrimp into the soup and heat through for 5 minutes or until the shrimp have changed color.

5 Transfer to a warmed soup tureen or individual warmed serving bowls and serve immediately.

NUTRITION
Calories 217; Sugars 16 g; Protein 16 g;
Carbohydrate 31 g; Fat 4 g; Saturates 1 g

very easy

10 mins

20 mins

🍴 **COOK'S TIP**

You could use Thai ginger or galangal, a member of the ginger family, instead of the gingerroot in this recipe. It is yellow in color with pink sprouts and a knobbly surface. The flavor is aromatic and less pungent than ginger.

Crab and corn are classic ingredients in Chinese cooking. Here, egg noodles are added for a filling dish.

Crab *and* Corn Soup

1 Heat the sunflower oil in a preheated wok or large, heavy-based pan.

2 Add the Chinese five-spice powder, carrots, corn, peas, scallions, and chile to the wok and cook for about 5 minutes, stirring constantly.

3 Add the crab meat to the wok and cook the mixture for 1 minute, distributing the crab meat evenly.

4 Roughly break up the egg noodles and add to the wok.

5 Pour the fish bouillon and soy sauce into the mixture in the wok and bring to a boil.

6 Cover the wok and let the soup simmer for 5 minutes.

7 Stir once more, then transfer the soup to a warmed soup tureen or individual warmed serving bowls and serve at once.

SERVES 4

1 tbsp sunflower oil
1 tsp Chinese five-spice powder
3 small carrots, cut into sticks
½ cup canned or frozen corn kernels
¾ cup frozen peas
6 scallions, trimmed and sliced
1 fresh red chile, seeded and very thinly sliced
14 oz/400 g canned white crab meat
6 oz/175 g egg noodles
7½ cups fish bouillon
3 tbsp soy sauce

NUTRITION
Calories *324*; Sugars *6 g*; Protein *27 g*; Carbohydrate *39 g*; Fat *8 g*; Saturates *2 g*

easy
5 mins
20 mins

 COOK'S TIP

Chinese five-spice powder is a mixture of star anise, fennel, cloves, cinnamon, and Szechuan pepper. It has an unmistakable flavor. Use it sparingly, as it is very pungent.

Thin strips of beef are marinated in soy sauce and garlic to form the basis of this delicious soup. Served with noodles, it is both filling and delicious.

Beef Noodle Soup

SERVES 4

8 oz/225 g lean beef
1 garlic clove, crushed
2 scallions, chopped
3 tbsp soy sauce
1 tsp sesame oil
8 oz/225 g egg noodles
3¾ cups beef bouillon
3 baby corn cobs, sliced
½ leek, shredded
4½ oz/125 g broccoli, cut into flowerets
pinch of chili powder

1 Using a sharp knife, cut the beef into thin strips and place in a large bowl with the garlic, scallions, soy sauce, and sesame oil.

2 Combine the ingredients in the bowl, turning the beef to coat. Cover and set aside to marinate in the refrigerator for 30 minutes.

3 Cook the noodles in a pan of boiling water for 3–4 minutes. Drain thoroughly and set aside.

4 Put the beef bouillon in a large pan and bring to a boil. Add the beef, with the marinade, the baby corn, shredded leek, and broccoli flowerets. Cover and simmer over low heat for 7–10 minutes or until the beef and vegetables are tender and cooked through.

5 Stir in the noodles and chili powder and cook for a further 2–3 minutes.

6 Transfer the soup to warmed bowls and serve immediately.

NUTRITION
Calories *186*; Sugars *1 g*; Protein *17 g*;
Carbohydrate *20 g*; Fat *5 g*; Saturates *1 g*

easy

35 mins

20 mins

(※) **COOK'S TIP**

Vary the vegetables used or use those to hand. If preferred, use a few drops of chili sauce instead of chili powder, but remember it is very hot!

In this recipe the pork is seasoned with traditional Chinese flavorings—soy sauce, rice wine vinegar, and a dash of sesame oil.

Chinese Potato *and* Pork Broth

1 Add the chicken bouillon, diced potatoes, and 1 tbsp of the vinegar to a pan and bring to a boil. Reduce the heat until the bouillon is just simmering.

2 Mix the cornstarch with the water then stir into the hot bouillon.

3 Bring the bouillon back to a boil, stirring until thickened, then reduce the heat until it is just simmering again.

4 Place the pork slices in a dish and season with the remaining rice wine vinegar, the soy sauce, and sesame oil.

5 Add the pork slices, carrot strips, and ginger to the bouillon and cook for 10 minutes. Stir in the scallions, red bell pepper, and bamboo shoots. Cook for a further 5 minutes. Pour the soup into warmed bowls and serve immediately.

SERVES 4

1 quart chicken bouillon
2 large potatoes, diced
2 tbsp rice wine vinegar
2 tbsp cornstarch
4 tbsp water
4½ oz/125 g pork fillet, sliced
1 tbsp light soy sauce
1 tsp sesame oil
1 carrot, cut into very thin strips
1 tsp gingerroot, chopped
3 scallions, sliced thinly
1 red bell pepper, sliced
8 oz/225 g canned bamboo shoots, drained

NUTRITION
Calories *166*; Sugars *2 g*; Protein *10 g*; Carbohydrate *26 g*; Fat *5 g*; Saturates *1 g*

 easy

5 mins

20 mins

🍴 COOK'S TIP

For extra heat, add 1 chopped red chile or 1 tsp of chili powder to the soup in step 5.

This meaty chili tastes lighter than one made with beef. Good for informal entertaining, the recipe is easily doubled.

Pork Chili Soup

SERVES 4

2 tsp olive oil
1 lb 2 oz/500 g lean ground pork
1 onion, chopped finely
1 celery stalk, chopped finely
1 bell pepper, seeded and finely chopped
2–3 garlic cloves, chopped finely
14 oz/400 g canned chopped tomatoes in juice
3 tbsp tomato paste
2 cups chicken or meat bouillon
¼ tsp ground coriander
¼ tsp ground cumin
¼ tsp dried oregano
1 tsp mild chili powder
salt and pepper
chopped fresh cilantro leaves or parsley, to garnish
sour cream, to serve

1 Heat the oil in a pan over medium-high heat. Add the pork, season with salt and pepper, and cook, stirring frequently, until no longer pink. Reduce the heat to medium and add the onion, celery, bell pepper, and garlic. Cover and cook, stirring occasionally, for a further 5 minutes or until the onion is softened.

2 Add the tomatoes, tomato paste, and the bouillon. Stir in the coriander, cumin, oregano, and chili powder. Season with salt and pepper to taste.

3 Bring just to a boil, then reduce the heat to low, cover, and simmer for about 30–40 minutes or until all the vegetables are very tender. Taste and adjust the seasoning, adding more chili powder if you like it hotter.

4 Ladle the chili into warmed bowls and sprinkle with chopped cilantro or parsley. You can either hand the sour cream separately or top each serving with a spoonful.

NUTRITION
Calories 308; Sugars 13 g; Protein 40 g; Carbohydrate 15 g; Fat 10 g; Saturates 3 g

easy
10 mins
50–60 mins

COOK'S TIP

For extra spicy heat you can replace the mild chili powder with fresh red or green chiles, chopped finely.

Steaming the meatballs over the soup gives added flavor to the broth. A bamboo steamer that rests on the top of a pan is useful for this recipe.

Asian Pork Balls *in* Broth

1 To make the pork balls, put the pork, spinach, scallions, and garlic in a bowl. Add the five-spice powder and soy sauce and mix until thoroughly combined.

2 Shape the pork mixture into 24 balls. Place them in a single layer in a steamer that will fit over the top of a pan or in a wok.

3 Bring the bouillon just to a boil in a pan or wok that will accommodate the steamer. Reduce the heat so that the liquid just bubbles gently. Add the mushrooms to the bouillon and place the steamer, covered, on top of the pan or wok. Steam for 10 minutes. Remove the steamer and set aside on a plate.

4 Add the bok choy or Napa cabbage and scallions to the pan or wok and cook gently in the bouillon for 3–4 minutes or until the greens are wilted. Season the broth to taste with salt and pepper.

5 Divide the pork balls evenly among 6 warmed bowls and ladle the soup over them. Serve immediately.

SERVES 6

4 cups chicken bouillon
1¼ cups thinly sliced shiitake mushrooms
6 oz/175 g bok choy or other Napa cabbage, sliced into thin ribbons
6 scallions, thinly sliced
salt and pepper

pork balls

8 oz/225 g lean ground pork
1 oz/25 g fresh spinach leaves, chopped finely
2 scallions, chopped finely
1 garlic clove, chopped very finely
pinch of Chinese five-spice powder
1 tsp soy sauce

NUTRITION

Calories *67*; Sugars *1 g*; Protein *9 g*; Carbohydrate *3 g*; Fat *2 g*; Saturates *1 g*

 moderate

 15 mins

15 mins

18 mins

This is a very filling soup, as it contains rice and tender pieces of lamb. Serve before a light main course.

Lamb *and* Rice Soup

SERVES 4

5½ oz/150 g lean lamb
¼ cup rice
3¾ cups lamb bouillon
1 leek, sliced
1 garlic clove, sliced thinly
2 tsp light soy sauce
1 tsp rice wine vinegar
1 medium open-cap mushroom, sliced thinly
salt

1 Using a sharp knife, trim any fat from the lamb and cut the meat into thin strips. Set aside until required.

2 Bring a large pan of lightly salted water to a boil and add the rice. Bring back to a boil, stir once, reduce the heat, and cook for 10–15 minutes or until the rice is tender.

3 Drain the rice, rinse under cold running water, drain again, and set aside until required.

4 Meanwhile, put the lamb bouillon in a large pan and bring to a boil.

5 Add the lamb strips, leek, garlic, soy sauce, and rice wine vinegar to the bouillon in the pan. Reduce the heat, cover, and leave to simmer for 10 minutes or until the lamb is tender and cooked through.

6 Add the mushroom slices and the rice to the pan and cook for a further 2–3 minutes or until the mushroom is completely cooked through.

7 Ladle the soup into 4 individual warmed soup bowls and serve immediately.

NUTRITION

Calories *116*; Sugars *0.2 g*; Protein *9 g*; Carbohydrate *12 g*; Fat *4 g*; Saturates *2 g*

easy

5 mins

35 mins

🍳 COOK'S TIP

Use a few dried Chinese mushrooms, rehydrated according to the packet instructions and chopped, as an alternative to the open-cap mushroom. Add the Chinese mushrooms with the lamb in step 4.

Packed with tomatoes, garbanzo beans, and vegetables, this thick and hearty entrée soup is bursting with exotic flavors and aromas.

Spicy Lamb Soup

1 Heat the oil in a large pan or flameproof casserole over medium-high heat. Add the lamb, in batches if necessary, and cook, stirring occasionally, until evenly browned on all sides, adding a little more oil if needed. Remove the meat, with a slotted spoon.

2 Reduce the heat and add the onion and garlic to the pan. Cook, stirring frequently, for 1–2 minutes.

3 Add the water and return all the meat to the pan. Bring just to a boil and skim off any foam that rises to the surface. Reduce the heat and stir in the tomatoes, bay leaf, thyme, oregano, cinnamon, cumin, turmeric, and harissa. Simmer for about 1 hour or until the meat is very tender. Discard the bay leaf.

4 Stir in the garbanzo beans, carrot, and potato and simmer for about 15 minutes. Add the zucchini and peas and simmer for a further 15–20 minutes or until all the vegetables are tender.

5 Season to taste with salt and pepper and add more harissa if desired. Ladle the soup into warmed bowls, garnish with fresh mint or cilantro, and serve immediately.

SERVES 4

1–2 tbsp olive oil
1 lb/450 g lean boneless lamb, trimmed of fat and cut into ½-inch/1-cm cubes
1 onion, chopped finely
2–3 garlic cloves, crushed
5 cups water
14 oz/400 g canned chopped tomatoes
1 bay leaf
½ tsp dried thyme
½ tsp dried oregano
pinch of ground cinnamon
¼ tsp ground cumin
¼ tsp ground turmeric
1 tsp harissa
14 oz/400 g canned garbanzo beans, rinsed and drained
1 carrot, diced
1 potato, diced
1 zucchini, quartered lengthwise and sliced
1 cup fresh or thawed frozen green peas
salt and pepper
fresh mint or cilantro leaves, to garnish

NUTRITION

Calories 323; Sugars 6 g; Protein 27 g; Carbohydrate 25 g; Fat 13 g; Saturates 4 g

✪✪✪ moderate

 10 mins

 1 hr 45 mins

Tender cooked chicken strips and baby corn cobs are the main flavors in this delicious clear soup, with just a hint of ginger.

Curried Chicken Soup

SERVES 4

1 cup canned corn, drained
3¾ cups chicken bouillon
12 oz/350 g cooked, lean chicken, cut into strips
16 baby corn cobs
1 tsp Chinese curry powder
½-inch/1-cm piece of fresh gingerroot, grated
3 tbsp light soy sauce
2 tbsp chopped fresh chives

1 Place the canned corn in a food processor, with ⅔ cup of the chicken bouillon and process until the mixture forms a smooth purée.

2 Pass the corn purée through a fine strainer, pressing with the back of a spoon to remove any husks.

3 Pour the remaining chicken bouillon into a large pan and add the strips of cooked chicken. Stir in the corn purée to combine well.

4 Add the baby corn cobs and bring the soup to a boil. Boil over medium heat for 10 minutes.

5 Add the Chinese curry powder, grated fresh gingerroot, and light soy sauce and stir well to combine. Cook for a further 10–15 minutes.

6 Stir in the chopped chives. Transfer the soup to warmed soup bowls and serve immediately.

NUTRITION
Calories *206*; Sugars *5 g*; Protein *29 g*;
Carbohydrate *13 g*; Fat *5 g*; Saturates *1 g*

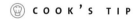 easy

 5 mins

 30 mins

🍳 **COOK'S TIP**

Prepare the soup up to 24 hours in advance without adding the chicken. Cool, cover, and store in the refrigerator. Add the chicken and heat the soup through thoroughly before serving.

This tasty chicken soup has the addition of poached eggs, making it both delicious and filling. Use fresh, homemade bouillon for a better flavour.

Clear Chicken *and* Egg Soup

1 Bring a large pan of water to a boil and add the salt and rice wine vinegar.

2 Reduce the heat so that it is just simmering and carefully break the eggs into the water, one at a time. Poach the eggs for 1 minute.

3 Remove the poached eggs with a slotted spoon and set aside.

4 Bring the chicken bouillon to a boil in a separate pan and add the leek, broccoli, chicken, mushrooms, and sherry and season with chili sauce to taste. Cook for 10–15 minutes.

5 Add the poached eggs to the soup and cook for a further 2 minutes. Carefully transfer the soup and poached eggs to 4 soup bowls. Dust with a little chili powder and serve immediately.

SERVES 4

1 tsp salt
1 tbsp rice wine vinegar
4 eggs
3¾ cups chicken bouillon
1 leek, sliced
4½ oz/125 g broccoli flowerets
1 cup shredded cooked chicken
2 open-cap mushrooms, sliced
1 tbsp dry sherry
dash of chili sauce
chili powder, to garnish

NUTRITION

Calories *138*; Sugars *1 g*; Protein *16 g*; Carbohydrate *1 g*; Fat *7 g*; Saturates *2 g*

 easy

 5 mins

35 mins

COOK'S TIP

You could use 4 dried Chinese mushrooms, rehydrated according to the packet instructions, instead of the open-cap mushrooms, if you prefer.

This filling soup is packed with spicy flavors and bright colors for a really attractive and hearty dish.

Spicy Chicken Noodle Soup

SERVES 4

2 tbsp tamarind paste
4 red chiles, chopped finely
2 cloves garlic, crushed
2 tsp finely chopped fresh gingerroot
4 tbsp fish sauce
2 tbsp palm sugar or superfine sugar
8 lime leaves, roughly torn
5 cups chicken bouillon
12 oz/350 g boneless chicken breast
3½ oz/100 g carrots, sliced thinly
12 oz/350 g sweet potato, diced
3½ oz/100 g baby corn cobs, halved
3 tbsp roughly chopped fresh cilantro
3½ oz/100 g cherry tomatoes, halved
5½ oz/150 g flat rice noodles
chopped fresh cilantro, to garnish

1 Preheat a large wok or skillet. Place the tamarind paste, chiles, garlic, ginger, fish sauce, sugar, lime leaves, and chicken bouillon in the wok and bring to a boil, stirring constantly. Reduce the heat and cook for about 5 minutes.

2 Using a sharp knife, thinly slice the chicken. Add the chicken to the wok and cook for a further 5 minutes, stirring the mixture well.

3 Reduce the heat and add the carrots, sweet potato, and baby corn cobs to the wok. Leave to simmer, uncovered, for 5 minutes or until the vegetables are just tender and the chicken is completely cooked through.

4 Stir in the chopped fresh cilantro, cherry tomatoes, and flat rice noodles.

5 Leave the soup to simmer for about 5 minutes or until the noodles are tender.

6 Garnish the spicy chicken noodle soup with chopped fresh cilantro and serve hot.

NUTRITION
Calories *286*; Sugars *21 g*; Protein *22 g*; Carbohydrate *37 g*; Fat *6 g*; Saturates *1 g*

 easy

 15 mins

 20 mins

COOK'S TIP

Tamarind paste is produced from the seed pod of the tamarind tree. It adds both a brown color and tang to soups and gravies. If unavailable, dilute molasses (dark muscovado) sugar or treacle with lime juice.

This fragrant soup combines citrus flavors with coconut and a hint of piquancy from chiles.

Chicken *and* Coconut Soup

1 Using a sharp knife, slice the chicken into thin strips.

2 Place the coconut in a heatproof bowl and pour over the boiling water. Work the coconut mixture through a strainer. Pour the coconut water into a large pan and add the bouillon.

3 Add the scallions to the pan. Slice the base of each lemon grass and discard damaged leaves. Bruise the stalks and add to the pan.

4 Peel the rind from the lime in large strips. Extract the juice and add to the pan with the lime strips, ginger, soy sauce, and coriander. Bruise the chiles with a fork then add to the pan. Heat the pan to just below boiling point.

5 Add the chicken and fresh cilantro to the pan, bring to a boil, then simmer for 10 minutes.

6 Discard the lemon grass, lime rind, and red chiles. Pour the blended cornstarch mixture into the pan and stir until slightly thickened. Season with salt and white pepper to taste and serve immediately, garnished with chopped red chile.

SERVES 4

1¾ cups cooked, skinned chicken breast
1⅓ cups unsweetened desiccated coconut
2 cups boiling water
2 cups Fresh Chicken Bouillon (see page 14)
4 scallions, white and green parts,
    sliced thinly
2 stalks lemon grass
1 lime
1 tsp grated gingerroot
1 tbsp light soy sauce
2 tsp ground coriander
2 large fresh red chiles
1 tbsp chopped fresh cilantro
1 tbsp cornstarch, mixed with 2 tbsp
    cold water
salt and white pepper
chopped red chile, to garnish

NUTRITION
Calories *345*; Sugars *2 g*; Protein *28 g*;
Carbohydrate *5 g*; Fat *24 g*; Saturates *18 g*

 moderate

2 hrs 15 mins

 15 mins

This soup makes a change from traditional chicken soup. It is spicy, and garnished with a generous quantity of cilantro leaves.

Thai-Style Chicken *and* Coconut Soup

SERVES 4

5 cups chicken bouillon
7 oz/200 g skinless boneless chicken
1 fresh chile, split lengthwise and seeded
3-inch/7.5-cm piece lemon grass, split lengthwise
3–4 lime leaves
1-inch/2.5-cm piece fresh gingerroot, peeled and sliced
½ cup coconut milk
6–8 scallions, sliced diagonally
¼ tsp chili paste, to taste
salt
fresh cilantro leaves, to garnish

1 Put the bouillon in a pan with the chicken, chile, lemon grass, lime leaves, and ginger. Bring almost to a boil, reduce the heat, cover and simmer for 20–25 minutes or until the chicken is cooked through and firm to the touch.

2 Remove the chicken from the pan and strain the bouillon. Set aside the chile and lime leaves. When the chicken is cool, slice thinly, or shred into bite-sized pieces.

3 Return the bouillon to the pan and heat to simmering. Stir in the coconut milk and scallions. Add the chicken and continue simmering for about 10 minutes or until the soup is heated through and the flavors have mingled.

4 Stir in the chili paste. Season to taste with salt and, if wished, add a little more chili paste.

5 Ladle into warmed bowls and float cilantro leaves, the chile, and the lime leaves on top to serve.

NUTRITION
Calories 76; Sugars 2 g; Protein 13 g;
Carbohydrate 3 g; Fat 1 g; Saturates 0 g

⭐⭐ easy
5 mins
40 mins

🍳 COOK'S TIP

Once the bouillon is flavored and the chicken cooked, this soup is very quick to finish. If you wish, poach the chicken and strain the bouillon ahead of time. Store in the refrigerator separately.

This well-known soup from Peking is easy to make and very filling. It is often eaten as a meal on its own and should be served before a light menu if it is offered as an appetizer.

Hot *and* Sour Soup

1 Blend the cornstarch with the water to form a smooth paste. Add the soy sauce, rice wine vinegar, pepper, and chili and mix together well.

2 Break the egg into a separate bowl and beat well.

3 Heat the oil in a preheated wok and cook the onion for 1–2 minutes.

4 Stir in the consommé, mushroom, and chicken and bring to a boil. Cook for about 15 minutes or until the chicken is tender.

5 Pour the cornstarch mixture into the soup and cook, stirring constantly, until it thickens.

6 As you are stirring, gradually drizzle the egg into the soup, to create threads of egg.

7 Sprinkle with the sesame oil and serve immediately.

SERVES 4

2 tbsp cornstarch
4 tbsp water
2 tbsp light soy sauce
3 tbsp rice wine vinegar
½ tsp ground black pepper
1 small fresh red chili, chopped finely
1 egg
2 tbsp vegetable oil
1 onion, chopped
3¾ cups chicken or beef consommé
1 open-cap mushroom, sliced
1¾ oz/50 g skinless chicken breast, cut into very thin strips
1 tsp sesame oil

NUTRITION
Calories *124*; Sugars *5 g*; Protein *1 g*; Carbohydrate *8 g*; Fat *8 g*; Saturates *1 g*

 moderate

10 mins

25 mins

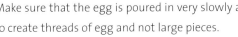 **COOK'S TIP**

Make sure that the egg is poured in very slowly and that you stir continuously to create threads of egg and not large pieces.

How delicious a simple, fresh soup can be. Chicken wings are good to use for making the bouillon, as the meat is very sweet and doesn't dry out.

Chicken Soup *with* Stars

SERVES 4

2 lb 12 oz/1.25 kg chicken pieces, such as wings or legs
2½ quarts water
1 celery stalk, sliced
1 large carrot, sliced
1 onion, sliced
1 leek, sliced
2 garlic cloves, crushed
8 peppercorns
4 allspice berries
3–4 parsley stems
2–3 fresh thyme sprigs
1 bay leaf
salt and pepper
¾ cup small pasta stars, or other very small shapes
chopped fresh parsley, to serve

1 Put the chicken in a large flameproof casserole with the water, celery, carrot, onion, leek, garlic, peppercorns, allspice, herbs, and ½ teaspoon salt. Bring just to a boil and skim off the foam that rises to the surface. Reduce the heat, partially cover, and simmer, for 2 hours.

2 Remove the chicken from the bouillon and set aside to cool. Continue simmering the bouillon, uncovered, for about 30 minutes. When the chicken is cool enough to handle, remove the meat from the bones and, if necessary, cut into bite-size pieces.

3 Strain the bouillon and remove as much fat as possible. Discard the vegetables and flavorings. (There should be about 7½ cups chicken bouillon.)

4 Bring the bouillon to a boil in a clean pan. Add the pasta and reduce the heat so that the bouillon boils very gently. Cook for about 10 minutes or until the pasta is tender, but still firm to the bite.

5 Stir in the chicken meat. Taste the soup and adjust the seasoning if necessary. Ladle into warmed bowls and serve sprinkled with parsley.

NUTRITION
Calories *119*; Sugars *2 g*; Protein *14 g*; Carbohydrate *13 g*; Fat *2 g*; Saturates *0 g*

 moderate

 20 mins

2 hrs 45 mins

This soup is a good way of using up leftover cooked chicken and rice. Any type of rice is suitable, from white or brown long-grain rice to wild rice.

Chicken *and* Rice Soup

1 Pour the bouillon into a large pan and add the carrots, celery, and leek. Bring to a boil, then reduce the heat to low, and simmer the bouillon gently, partially covered, for 10 minutes.

2 Stir in the peas, rice, and chicken, and continue cooking for another 10–15 minutes or until the vegetables are tender.

3 Add the chopped tarragon and parsley, then taste and adjust the seasoning, adding salt and pepper as needed.

4 Ladle the soup into warmed bowls, garnish with parsley and serve.

SERVES 4

6¾ cups Chicken Bouillon (see page 14)
2 small carrots, sliced very thinly
1 celery stalk, finely diced
1 baby leek, halved lengthwise and
   sliced thinly
4 oz/115 g tiny peas, defrosted if frozen
3 cups cooked rice
5½ oz/150 g cooked chicken, sliced
2 tsp chopped fresh tarragon
1 tbsp chopped fresh parsley
salt and pepper
fresh parsley sprigs, to garnish

NUTRITION
Calories *165*; Sugars *3 g*; Protein *14 g*;
Carbohydrate *19 g*; Fat *4 g*; Saturates *1 g*

 very easy

 25 mins

 30 mins

COOK'S TIP

If the bouillon you are using is a little on the weak side, or if you have used a bouillon cube, add the herbs at the beginning, so that they can flavor the bouillon for a longer time.

This is a hearty and robustly flavored soup, containing pieces of duck and vegetables cooked in a rich bouillon.

Peking Duck Soup

SERVES 4

4 oz/115 g lean duck breast meat
8 oz/225 g Napa cabbage
3¾ cups chicken or duck bouillon
1 tbsp dry sherry or Chinese rice wine
1 tbsp light soy sauce
2 garlic cloves, crushed
pinch of ground star anise
1 tbsp sesame seeds
1 tsp sesame oil
1 tbsp chopped fresh parsley

1 Remove the skin from the duck breast and finely dice the flesh. Using a sharp knife, shred the Napa cabbage.

2 Put the bouillon in a large pan and bring to a boil over medium heat. Add the sherry or rice wine, soy sauce, diced duck meat, and shredded Napa cabbage and stir thoroughly. Reduce the heat and simmer gently for 15 minutes.

3 Stir in the garlic and star anise and cook over a low heat for a further 10–15 minutes or until the duck is tender.

4 Meanwhile, dry-fry the sesame seeds in a preheated, heavy skillet or wok, stirring constantly, until they give off their fragrance.

5 Remove the sesame seeds from the skillet and stir them into the soup, with the sesame oil and the chopped fresh parsley.

6 Ladle the Peking duck soup into warmed bowls and serve immediately.

NUTRITION
Calories *92*; Sugars *3 g*; Protein *8 g*;
Carbohydrate *3 g*; Fat *5 g*; Saturates *1 g*

moderate

5 mins

35 mins

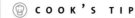 **COOK'S TIP**

If Napa cabbage is unavailable, use leafy green cabbage instead. You may wish to adjust the quantity to taste, as ordinary green cabbage has a stronger flavor and aroma than Napa cabbage.

This soup combines delicate flavors with a satisfying meaty taste. Although duck is notoriously fatty, the legs are leaner than the breast.

Asian Duck Broth

1 Put the duck in a large pan with the water. Bring just to a boil and skim off the foam that rises to the surface. Add the bouillon, ginger, carrot, onion, leek, garlic, peppercorns, and soy sauce. Reduce the heat, partially cover, and simmer gently for 1½ hours.

2 Remove the duck from the bouillon and set aside. When the duck is cool enough to handle, remove the meat from the bones, and slice thinly or shred into bite-size pieces, discarding any fat.

3 Strain the bouillon and press with the back of a spoon to extract all the liquid. Remove as much fat as possible. Discard the vegetables and flavorings.

4 Bring the bouillon just to a boil in a clean pan and add the strips of carrot and leek and the mushrooms with the duck meat. Reduce the heat and simmer gently for 5 minutes or until the carrot is just tender.

5 Stir in the watercress leaves and continue simmering for 1–2 minutes or until they are wilted. Taste the soup and adjust the seasoning if necessary, adding a little more soy sauce if desired. Ladle the soup into warmed soup bowls and then serve immediately.

SERVES 4

2 duck leg quarters, skinned
4 cups water
2½ cups chicken bouillon
1-inch/2.5-cm piece of fresh gingerroot, sliced
1 large carrot, sliced
1 onion, sliced
1 leek, sliced
3 garlic cloves, crushed
1 tsp black peppercorns
2 tbsp soy sauce
1 small carrot, cut into thin strips or slivers
1 small leek, cut into thin strips or slivers
1½ cups thinly sliced shiitake mushrooms
1 oz/25 g watercress leaves
salt and pepper

NUTRITION
Calories 98; Sugars 4 g; Protein 9 g; Carbohydrate 9 g; Fat 3 g; Saturates 1 g

 easy
 10 mins
1 hr 45 mins

European Soups

Soups are an important part of European cuisine and vary in content from hearty bean concoctions suitable for the coldest winter's day to creamy Vichyssoise and meaty stews. In this chapter there are nourishing lentil soup recipes, variations on Minestrone soup, and thick fish soups. Dishes are from France, including Provence and Brittany, Hungary, and there is a delicious lemony-flavored bean soup from Greece. Many of these soups are suitable for a main-course meal when combined with delicious freshly baked bread.

Plum tomatoes are ideal for making soups and sauces as they have denser, less watery flesh than rounder varieties.

Tomato *and* Pasta Soup

SERVES 4

4 tbsp sweet butter
1 large onion, chopped
2½ cups vegetable bouillon
2 lb/900 g Italian plum tomatoes, peeled and roughly chopped
pinch of baking soda
3 cups dried fusilli
1 tbsp superfine sugar
⅔ cup heavy cream
salt and pepper
fresh basil leaves, to garnish

1 Melt the butter in a large pan, add the chopped onion, and cook for 3 minutes, stirring. Add 1½ cups of the vegetable bouillon to the pan, with the chopped tomatoes and baking soda. Bring the soup to a boil and simmer for 20 minutes.

2 Remove the pan from the heat and let the soup cool a little. Purée the soup in a blender or food processor and then pour it through a fine strainer back into the pan.

3 Add the remaining vegetable bouillon and the fusilli to the pan, and season to taste with salt and pepper.

4 Add the sugar to the pan, bring to a boil, then reduce the heat and simmer for about 15 minutes.

5 Pour the soup into a warmed tureen or individual warmed bowls, swirl the heavy cream around the surface of the soup, and garnish with fresh basil leaves. Serve immediately.

NUTRITION
Calories *503*; Sugars *16 g*; Protein *9 g*;
Carbohydrate *59 g*; Fat *28 g*; Saturates *17 g*

 easy

5 mins

50–55 mins

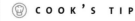 **COOK'S TIP**

To make orange and tomato soup, simply use half the quantity of vegetable bouillon, topped up with the same amount of fresh orange juice, and garnish the soup with orange zest.

This Spanish soup is full of chopped and grated vegetables with a puréed tomato base. It requires chilling, so prepare well in advance.

Gazpacho

1 Coarsely grate the cucumber into a large bowl and add the chopped green bell pepper.

2 Put the tomatoes, onion, and garlic in a food processor or blender, add the oil, vinegar, lemon or lime juice, and tomato paste and process until a smooth purée is formed. Alternatively, finely chop the tomatoes and finely grate the onion, then mix together and add the crushed garlic, oil, vinegar, lemon or lime juice, and tomato paste.

3 Add the tomato mixture to the bowl and mix well, then add the tomato juice and mix again.

4 Season to taste, cover the bowl with plastic wrap and chill thoroughly—for at least 6 hours and preferably longer so that the flavors have time to blend.

5 Prepare the side dishes of chopped green bell pepper, thinly sliced onion rings, and garlic croûtons and arrange them in individual serving bowls.

6 Ladle the soup into bowls, preferably from a soup tureen set in the center of the table with the side dishes of bell pepper, onion rings, and croûtons placed around it. Hand the dishes round to allow the guests to help themselves.

SERVES 4

½ small cucumber
½ small green bell pepper, seeded and very finely chopped
1 lb/450 g ripe tomatoes, peeled or 2 cups canned chopped tomatoes
½ onion, chopped coarsely
2–3 garlic cloves, crushed
3 tbsp olive oil
2 tbsp white wine vinegar
1–2 tbsp lemon or lime juice
2 tbsp tomato paste
1¾ cups tomato juice
salt and pepper

to serve
chopped green bell pepper
thinly sliced onion rings
garlic croûtons (see page 89)

NUTRITION
Calories *140*; Sugars *12 g*; Protein *3 g*; Carbohydrate *13 g*; Fat *9 g*; Saturates *1 g*

 very easy

6 hrs 30 mins

 0 mins

A delicious creamy soup with grated carrot and chopped parsley for texture and color. Serve with crusty cheese biscuits for a hearty lunch.

Thick Onion Soup

SERVES 6

¹/₃ cup butter
1 lb/450 g onions, chopped finely
1 garlic clove, crushed
¹/₃ cup all-purpose flour
2¹/₂ cups vegetable bouillon
2¹/₂ cups milk
2–3 tsp lemon or lime juice
good pinch of ground allspice
1 bay leaf
1 carrot, coarsely grated
4–6 tbsp heavy cream
2 tbsp chopped parsley
salt and pepper

cheese biscuits

1¹/₃ cups malted wheat or whole-wheat flour
2 tsp baking powder
¹/₄ cup butter
4 tbsp grated Parmesan cheese
1 egg, beaten
about ¹/₃ cup milk

NUTRITION
Calories 277; Sugars 12 g; Protein 6 g;
Carbohydrate 19 g; Fat 20 g; Saturates 8 g

easy

20 mins

1 hr 10 mins

1 Melt the butter in a pan and cook the onions and garlic over low heat, stirring frequently, for 10–15 minutes or until soft, but not colored. Stir in the flour and cook, stirring, for 1 minute, then gradually stir in the bouillon and bring to a boil, stirring frequently. Add the milk, then bring back to a boil.

2 Season to taste with salt and pepper and add 2 teaspoons of the lemon or lime juice, the allspice, and the bay leaf. Cover and simmer for about 25 minutes or until the vegetables are tender. Discard the bay leaf.

3 Meanwhile, make the biscuits. Combine the flour, baking powder, and seasoning and rub in the butter until the mixture resembles fine bread crumbs. Stir in 3 tablespoons of the cheese, the egg, and enough milk to mix to a soft dough.

4 Shape into a bar about ³/₄ inch/2 cm thick. Place on a floured cookie sheet and mark into slices. Sprinkle with the remaining cheese and bake in a preheated oven, 425°F/220°C, for about 20 minutes or until risen and a golden brown color.

5 Stir the carrot into the soup and simmer for 2–3 minutes. Add more lemon or lime juice, if necessary. Stir in the cream and reheat. Garnish and serve with the warm biscuits.

Fresh pesto is a treat for the taste buds and very different in flavor from that available from supermarkets. Store fresh pesto in the refrigerator.

Potato *and* Pesto Soup

1 To make the pesto, put all of the ingredients in a blender or food processor and process for 2 minutes, or blend by hand using a pestle and mortar.

2 Finely chop the bacon, potatoes, and onions. Fry the bacon in the oil in a large pan over a medium heat for 4 minutes. Add the butter, potatoes, and onions and cook for 12 minutes, stirring constantly.

3 Add the bouillon and milk to the pan, bring to a boil, and simmer for 10 minutes. Add the conchigliette and simmer for a further 10–12 minutes.

4 Blend in the cream and simmer for 5 minutes. Add the parsley, salt, and pepper and 2 tbsp pesto sauce. Transfer the soup to warmed serving bowls and serve with Parmesan cheese and fresh garlic bread.

SERVES 4

3 slices rindless, smoked, fatty bacon
1 lb/450 g floury potatoes
1 lb/450 g onions
2 tbsp olive oil
2 tbsp butter
2½ cups chicken bouillon
2½ cups milk
3½ oz/100 g dried conchigliette
⅔ cup double cream
chopped fresh parsley
salt and pepper
freshly grated Parmesan cheese and garlic bread, to serve

pesto sauce
1 cup finely chopped fresh parsley
2 garlic cloves, crushed
⅔ cup pine nuts, crushed
2 tbsp chopped fresh basil leaves
½ cup freshly grated Parmesan cheese
white pepper
⅔ cup olive oil

NUTRITION

Calories *548*; Sugars *0 g*; Protein *11 g*; Carbohydrate *10 g*; Fat *52 g*; Saturates *18 g*

 easy

 5–10 mins

50 mins

This creamy soup has
a delightful pale green
coloring and rich flavor
from the blend of tender
broccoli and blue cheese.

Broccoli *and* Potato Soup

SERVES 4

2 tbsp olive oil
1 lb/450 g potatoes, diced
1 onion, diced
8 oz/225 g broccoli flowerets
4½ oz/125 g blue cheese, crumbled
1 quart vegetable bouillon
⅔ cup heavy cream
pinch of paprika
salt and pepper

1 Heat the oil in a large pan. Add the potatoes and onion. Cook, stirring constantly, for 5 minutes.

2 Reserve a few broccoli flowerets for the garnish and add the remaining broccoli to the pan. Add the cheese and the vegetable bouillon.

3 Bring to a boil, then reduce the heat, cover the pan, and simmer for 25 minutes or until the potatoes are tender.

4 Transfer the soup to a food processor or blender in batches and process until the mixture is smooth. Alternatively, press the vegetables through a strainer with the back of a wooden spoon.

5 Return the purée to a clean pan and stir in the heavy cream and a pinch of paprika. Season to taste with salt and pepper.

6 Blanch the reserved broccoli flowerets in a little boiling water for about 2 minutes, then lift them out of the pan with a slotted spoon.

7 Pour the soup into warmed individual bowls and garnish with the broccoli flowerets and a sprinkling of paprika. Serve the soup immediately.

NUTRITION
Calories *452*; Sugars *4 g*; Protein *14 g*;
Carbohydrate *20 g*; Fat *35 g*; Saturates *19 g*

 moderate

5–10 mins

35 mins

 COOK'S TIP

This soup freezes very successfully. Follow the method described here up to step 4, and freeze the soup after it has been puréed. Add the cream and paprika just before serving. Garnish and serve.

This refreshing chilled soup is ideal for alfresco dining. It is very quick to make, but needs several hours in the refrigerator to chill thoroughly.

Onion *and* Artichoke Soup

1 Heat the oil in a large pan and cook the chopped onion and crushed garlic until just soft.

2 Using a sharp knife, coarsely chop the artichoke hearts. Add the artichoke pieces to the onion and garlic mixture in the pan. Pour in the hot bouillon, stirring.

3 Bring the mixture to a boil, then reduce the heat, and let simmer, covered, for about 3 minutes.

4 Place the mixture in a food processor and blend until smooth. Alternatively, push the mixture through a strainer to remove any lumps.

5 Return the soup to the pan. Stir the light cream and fresh thyme into the soup.

6 Transfer the soup to a large bowl and cover, and then let chill in the refrigerator for about 3–4 hours.

7 Transfer the chilled soup to warmed individual soup bowls and garnish with strips of sun-dried tomato. Serve with lots of fresh, crusty bread.

SERVES 4

1 tbsp olive oil
1 onion, chopped
1 garlic clove, crushed
28 oz/800 g canned artichoke hearts, drained
2½ cups hot vegetable bouillon
⅔ cup light cream
2 tbsp fresh thyme, stalks removed
2 sun-dried tomatoes, cut into strips

NUTRITION

Calories *159*; Sugars *2 g*; Protein *2 g*; Carbohydrate *5 g*; Fat *15 g*; Saturates *6 g*

 ⭐⭐⭐   moderate

🕐   5 mins

🕐   15 mins

👨‍🍳 COOK'S TIP

Try adding 2 tablespoons of dry vermouth, such as Martini, to the soup in step 5.

Mediterranean vegetables, roasted in olive oil and flavored with a pinch of thyme, are the basis for this delicious soup.

Roasted Vegetable Soup

SERVES 6

2–3 tbsp olive oil

1½ lb/675 g ripe tomatoes, peeled, cored, and halved

3 large yellow bell peppers, halved, cored, and seeded

3 zucchini, halved lengthwise

1 small eggplant, halved lengthwise

4 garlic cloves, halved

2 onions, cut into eighths

pinch of dried thyme

4 cups vegetable bouillon

½ cup light cream

salt and pepper

shredded basil leaves, to garnish

NUTRITION
Calories *163*; Sugars *13 g*; Protein *5 g*;
Carbohydrate *15 g*; Fat *10 g*; Saturates *3 g*

★★★   moderate

15 mins

1 hr 15 mins

1 Brush a large shallow baking dish with olive oil. Laying them cut-side down, arrange the tomatoes, bell peppers, zucchini, and eggplant in one layer (use two dishes, if necessary). Tuck the garlic cloves and onion pieces into the gaps and drizzle the vegetables with olive oil. Season lightly with salt and pepper and sprinkle with the thyme.

2 Place in a preheated oven at 375°F/ 190°C and bake the vegetables, uncovered, for 30–35 minutes or until they are soft and browned around the edges. Let cool, then scrape out the eggplant flesh and remove the skin from the bell peppers.

3 Working in batches, put the eggplant and bell pepper flesh, together with the zucchini, into a food processor and chop to the consistency of salsa or pickle; do not purée. Alternatively, place in a bowl and chop together with a knife.

4 Combine the bouillon and chopped vegetable mixture in a pan and simmer over medium heat for about 20–30 minutes or until all the vegetables are tender and the flavors have completely blended.

5 Stir the cream into the soup and simmer over low heat for about 5 minutes, stirring occasionally, until hot. Taste and adjust the seasoning, if necessary. Ladle the soup into warmed bowls, garnish with basil, and serve.

This is a classic creamy soup made from potatoes and leeks. To achieve the delicate pale color, be sure to use only the white parts of the leeks.

Vichyssoise

1 Trim the leeks and remove most of the green part. Slice the white part of the leeks very finely.

2 Melt the butter or margarine in a pan. Add the leeks and onion and sauté, stirring occasionally, for about 5 minutes without browning.

3 Add the potatoes, vegetable bouillon, lemon juice, nutmeg, coriander, and bay leaf to the pan. Season to taste with salt and pepper and bring to a boil. Cover and simmer for about 30 minutes or until all the vegetables are very soft.

4 Cool the soup a little. Remove and discard the bay leaf and then press through a strainer or process in a food processor or blender until smooth. Pour into a clean pan.

5 Blend the egg yolk into the cream. Add a little of the soup to this mixture and then whisk it all back into the soup. Reheat the soup gently, without boiling. Adjust the seasoning to taste if necessary. Cool, and then chill thoroughly in the refrigerator.

6 Serve the chilled soup garnished with a sprinkling of freshly snipped chives.

SERVES 6

3 large leeks
3 tbsp butter or margarine
1 onion, sliced thinly
1 lb 2 oz/500 g potatoes, chopped
3½ cups vegetable bouillon
2 tsp lemon juice
pinch of ground nutmeg
¼ tsp ground coriander
1 bay leaf
1 egg yolk
⅔ cup light cream
salt and white pepper
freshly snipped chives, to garnish

NUTRITION
Calories *208*; Sugars *5 g*; Protein *5 g*;
Carbohydrate *20 g*; Fat *12 g*; Saturates *6 g*

very easy

10 mins

40 mins

This robust stew is full of Mediterranean flavors. If you do not want to prepare the fish yourself, ask your local fish store to do it for you.

Italian Fish Stew

SERVES 4

2 tbsp olive oil
2 red onions, chopped finely
1 garlic clove, crushed
2 zucchini, sliced
14 oz/400 g canned chopped tomatoes
3¾ cups fish or vegetable bouillon
¾ cup dried pasta shapes
12 oz/350 g firm white fish, such as cod, haddock, or hake
1 tbsp chopped fresh basil or oregano or 1 tsp dried oregano
1 tsp grated lemon zest
1 tbsp cornstarch
1 tbsp water
salt and pepper
fresh basil or oregano sprigs, to garnish

1 Heat the oil in a large pan. Add the onions and garlic and cook over low heat, stirring occasionally, for about 5 minutes or until softened. Add the zucchini and cook, stirring frequently, for 2–3 minutes.

2 Add the tomatoes and bouillon to the pan and bring to a boil. Add the pasta, bring back to a boil, reduce the heat, and cover. Simmer for 5 minutes.

3 Skin and bone the fish, then cut it into chunks. Add to the pan with the basil or oregano and lemon zest and simmer gently for 5 minutes or until the fish is opaque and flakes easily (take care not to overcook it) and the pasta is tender, but still firm to the bite.

4 Blend the cornstarch with the water to a smooth paste and stir into the stew. Cook gently for 2 minutes, stirring constantly, until thickened. Season with salt and pepper to taste.

5 Ladle the stew into 4 warmed soup bowls. Garnish with basil or oregano sprigs and serve immediately.

NUTRITION

Calories 236; Sugars 4 g; Protein 20 g;
Carbohydrate 25 g; Fat 7 g; Saturates 1 g

 moderate

5–10 mins

25 mins

For the best results, you need to use flavorful fish, such as cod or haddock, for this recipe. Frozen fish fillets are also suitable.

Provençal Fish Soup

1 Heat the oil in a large pan over medium heat. Add the onions and cook, stirring occasionally, for about 5 minutes or until softened. Add the leek, carrot, celery, fennel, if using, and garlic and continue cooking for 4–5 minutes or until the leek is wilted.

2 Add the wine and simmer for 1 minute. Add the tomatoes, bay leaf, fennel seeds, orange zest, saffron, and water. Bring just to a boil, reduce the heat, cover, and simmer gently, stirring occasionally, for 30 minutes.

3 Add the fish and cook for a further 20–30 minutes or until it flakes easily. Remove the bay leaf and orange rind.

4 Remove the pan from the heat and set aside to cool slightly, then transfer to a blender or food processor, and process to a smooth purée, working in batches if necessary. (If using a food processor, strain off the cooking liquid and reserve. Purée the soup solids with enough cooking liquid to moisten them, then combine with the remaining liquid.)

5 Return the soup to the pan. Taste and adjust the seasoning, if necessary, and simmer for 5–10 minutes or until heated through. Ladle the soup into warmed bowls and sprinkle with croûtons, if using. Serve.

SERVES 4

1 tbsp olive oil
2 onions, chopped finely
1 small leek, sliced thinly
1 small carrot, chopped finely
1 celery stalk, chopped finely
1 small fennel bulb, chopped finely (optional)
3 garlic cloves, chopped finely
1 cup dry white wine
14 oz/400 g canned tomatoes
1 bay leaf
pinch of fennel seeds
2 strips of orange zest
1/4 tsp saffron threads
5 cups water
12 oz/350 g white fish fillets, skinned
salt and pepper
croûtons, to serve (optional)

NUTRITION
Calories 122; Sugars 6 g; Protein 12 g; Carbohydrate 7 g; Fat 3 g; Saturates 0 g

 moderate

10 mins

 1 hr 30 mins

The delicate color of this soup belies its heady flavors. The recipe has been adapted from a French soup thickened with a garlic mayonnaise.

Garlic Fish Soup

SERVES 4

2 tsp olive oil
1 large onion, chopped
1 small fennel bulb, chopped
1 leek, sliced
3–4 large garlic cloves, sliced thinly
½ cup dry white wine
5 cups fish bouillon
4 tbsp white rice
1 strip lemon zest
1 bay leaf
1 lb/450 g skinless white fish fillets, cut into
    1½-inch/4-cm pieces
¼ cup heavy cream
2 tbsp chopped fresh parsley
salt and pepper

1 Heat the oil in a large pan over a medium-low heat. Add the onion, fennel, leek, and garlic, and then cook for 4–5 minutes, stirring frequently, until the onion is softened.

2 Add the wine and bubble briefly. Add the fish bouillon, rice, lemon zest, and bay leaf. Bring the mixture to a boil, then reduce the heat to medium-low and simmer for 20–25 minutes or until the rice and vegetables are soft. Remove the lemon zest and bay leaf.

3 Let the soup cool slightly, then transfer to a blender or a food processor and process until smooth, working in batches if necessary. (If using a food processor, strain off the cooking liquid and reserve. Blend the soup solids with enough cooking liquid to moisten them, then combine with the remaining liquid.)

4 Return the blended soup to the pan and bring to a simmer. Add the fish pieces to the soup, then cover and continue simmering gently on a low heat, stirring occasionally, for 4–5 minutes or until the fish is cooked and begins to flake.

5 Stir in the cream. Taste and adjust the seasoning, adding salt, if needed, and pepper. Ladle into warmed soup bowls and serve sprinkled with parsley.

NUTRITION
Calories *191*; Sugars *4 g*; Protein *19 g*;
Carbohydrate *12 g*; Fat *7 g*; Saturates *3 g*

easy

5 mins

40–45 mins

Fishermen's soups are variable, depending on the season and the catch. Monkfish has a texture like lobster, but tender cod is equally appealing.

Breton Fish Soup *with* Cider

1 Melt the butter in a large pan over a medium-low heat. Add the leek and shallots and cook for about 5 minutes, stirring frequently, until they start to soften. Add the cider and bring to a boil.

2 Stir in the bouillon, potatoes, and bay leaf with a large pinch of salt (unless the bouillon is salty) and bring back to a boil. Reduce the heat, cover the pan, and cook the soup gently for 10 minutes.

3 Put the flour in a small bowl and very slowly whisk in a few tablespoons of the milk to make a thick paste. Stir in more milk, if needed, to make a smooth liquid.

4 Adjust the heat so that the soup bubbles gently. Stir in the flour mixture and cook, stirring frequently, for 5 minutes. Add the remaining milk and half the cream. Continue cooking for about 10 minutes or until the potatoes are tender.

5 Chop the sorrel finely and combine with the remaining cream. (If using a food processor, add the sorrel and chop, then add the cream and process briefly.)

6 Stir the sorrel cream into the soup and add the fish. Continue cooking, stirring occasionally, for about 3 minutes or until the monkfish stiffens or the cod just begins to flake. Taste the soup and adjust the seasoning, if necessary. Ladle into warmed bowls and serve.

SERVES 4

2 tsp butter
1 large leek, sliced thinly
2 shallots, chopped finely
1¼ cups hard cider
½ cup fish bouillon
9 oz/250 g potatoes, diced
1 bay leaf
4 tbsp all-purpose flour
¾ cup milk
¾ cup heavy cream
2 oz/55 g fresh sorrel leaves
12 oz/350 g skinless monkfish or cod fillet, cut into 1-inch/2.5-cm pieces
salt and pepper

NUTRITION
Calories *103*; Sugars *1.5 g*; Protein *5.2 g*; Carbohydrate *6.6 g*; Fat *6 g*; Saturates *3.8 g*

 moderate

5–10 mins

40 mins

This soup can be made in stages, so it is ideal for entertaining because some of it can be prepared in advance.

Mussel *and* Potato Soup

SERVES 4

2 lb 4 oz/1 kg mussels
10½ oz/300 g potatoes
3 tbsp all-purpose flour
2½ cups milk
1¼ cups whipping cream
1–2 garlic cloves, chopped finely
6 cups curly parsley leaves (1 large bunch)
salt and pepper

NUTRITION
Calories *95*; Sugars *2 g*; Protein *4 g*;
Carbohydrate *6 g*; Fat *6 g*; Saturates *4 g*

    easy

    15 mins

    45 mins

1 Discard any broken mussels and open shells that do not close. Rinse, pull off any "beards," and scrape off barnacles. Put the mussels in a large heavy-based pan. Cover tightly and cook over a high heat for about 4 minutes or until the mussels are open.

2 Remove the mussels from the shells, adding any additional juices to the pan. Strain the cooking liquid into a bowl through a cheesecloth-lined strainer and set aside.

3 Boil the potatoes, in their skins, in salted water for about 15 minutes or until tender. When cool enough to handle, peel and cut into small dice.

4 Mix the flour with a few tablespoons of the milk to make a smooth liquid.

5 Put the remaining milk, cream, and garlic in a pan and bring to a boil. Whisk in the flour mixture. Reduce the heat to medium-low and simmer for about 15 minutes or until the liquid has thickened slightly. Add the parsley and cook for about 2–3 minutes or until bright green and wilted.

6 Allow the soup base to cool slightly, then transfer to a blender or food processor and purée until smooth, working in batches if necessary.

7 Return the purée to the pan and stir in the mussel cooking liquid and the potatoes. Season to taste with salt, if needed, and pepper. Simmer the soup gently for 5–7 minutes. Add the mussels and continue cooking for about 2 minutes or until the soup is steaming and the mussels are hot. Ladle the soup into warmed bowls and serve.

This colorful mixed seafood soup would be superbly complemented by a dry white wine.

Italian Fish Soup

1 Melt the butter in a large pan, add the fish fillets, seafood, crabmeat, and onion, and cook gently over a low heat for 6 minutes.

2 Add the flour to the mixture, stirring thoroughly to avoid any lumps.

3 Gradually add the fish bouillon, stirring constantly, until the soup comes to a boil. Reduce the heat and simmer for 30 minutes.

4 Add the pasta to the pan and cook for an additional 10 minutes.

5 Stir in the anchovy paste, orange zest, orange juice, sherry, and heavy cream. Season to taste.

6 Heat the soup until completely warmed through. Transfer the soup to a tureen or to warmed soup bowls and serve with crusty brown bread.

SERVES 4

4 tbsp butter
1 lb/450 g assorted fish fillets, such as
    sea bass and snapper
1 lb/450 g prepared seafood, such as
    squid and shrimp
8 oz/225 g fresh crabmeat
1 large onion, sliced
¼ cup all-purpose flour
5 cups fish bouillon
¾ cup dried pasta shapes, such as
    ditalini or elbow macaroni
1 tbsp anchovy paste
grated zest and juice of 1 orange
¼ cup dry sherry
1¼ cups heavy cream
salt and black pepper
crusty brown bread, to serve

NUTRITION
Calories *668*; Sugars *3 g*; Protein *48 g*;
Carbohydrate *21 g*; Fat *43 g*; Saturates *25 g*

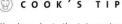 moderate

 5 mins

 55 mins

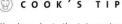 COOK'S TIP

The heads, tails, trimmings, and bones of virtually any non-oily fish can be used to make fish bouillon.

Wild mushrooms are available commercially and an increasing range of cultivated varieties is now to be found in many supermarkets.

Veal *and* Wild Mushroom Soup

SERVES 4

1 lb/450 g veal, sliced thinly
1 lb/450 g veal bones
5 cups water
1 small onion
6 peppercorns
1 tsp cloves
pinch of mace
5 oz/140 g oyster and shiitake mushrooms, chopped roughly
²⁄₃ cup heavy cream
³⁄₄ cup dried vermicelli
1 tbsp cornstarch
3 tbsp milk
salt and pepper

1 Put the veal, bones, and water into a large pan. Bring to a boil and reduce the heat. Add the onion, peppercorns, cloves, and mace and simmer for about 3 hours or until the veal bouillon is reduced by one-third.

2 Strain the bouillon, skim off any fat on the surface with a slotted spoon, and pour the bouillon into a clean pan. Add the veal meat to the pan.

3 Add the mushrooms and cream, bring to a boil over a low heat, and then leave to simmer for 12 minutes, stirring occasionally.

4 Meanwhile, cook the vermicelli in lightly salted boiling water for 10 minutes or until tender, but still firm to the bite. Drain and keep warm.

5 Mix the cornstarch and milk to form a smooth paste. Stir into the soup to thicken. Season to taste with salt and pepper and just before serving, add the vermicelli. Transfer the soup to a warmed tureen and serve immediately.

NUTRITION
Calories *413*; Sugars *3 g*; Protein *28 g*;
Carbohydrate *28 g*; Fat *22 g*; Saturates *12 g*

 moderate

5 mins

3 hrs 15 mins

🍴 **COOK'S TIP**

You can make this soup with the more inexpensive cuts of veal, such as breast or neck slices. These are lean and the long cooking time ensures that the meat is really tender.

Veal and ham is a classic combination, complemented here with the addition of sherry to create a richly-flavored Italian soup.

Veal *and* Ham Soup

1 Melt the butter in a large pan. Add the onions, carrot, celery, veal, and ham and cook over a low heat for 6 minutes.

2 Sprinkle over the flour and cook, stirring constantly, for a further 2 minutes. Gradually stir in the bouillon, then add the bay leaf, peppercorns, and salt. Bring to a boil and simmer for 1 hour.

3 Remove the pan from the heat and add the redcurrant jelly and cream sherry, stirring to combine. Set aside for about 4 hours.

4 Remove the bay leaf from the pan and discard. Reheat the soup over a very low heat until warmed through.

5 Meanwhile, cook the vermicelli in a pan of lightly salted boiling water for 10–12 minutes. Stir the vermicelli into the soup and transfer to warmed soup bowls. Garnish with garlic croûtons and serve.

S E R V E S   4

4 tbsp butter
1 onion, diced
1 carrot, diced
1 celery stalk, diced
1 lb/450 g veal, sliced very thinly
1 lb/450 g ham, sliced thinly
½ cup all-purpose flour
4 cups beef bouillon
1 bay leaf
8 black peppercorns
pinch of salt
3 tbsp redcurrant jelly
⅔ cup cream sherry
¾ cup dried vermicelli
garlic croûtons (see Cook's Tip), to serve

N U T R I T I O N
Calories *501*; Sugars *10 g*; Protein *38 g*;
Carbohydrate *28 g*; Fat *18 g*; Saturates *10 g*

   moderate

4 hrs 5 mins

1 hr 30 mins

 C O O K ' S   T I P

To make garlic croûtons, cut 3 slices of day-old crustless white bread into small cubes. Stir-fry 1–2 chopped garlic cloves in 3 tbsp oil for 1–2 minutes. Remove the garlic and cook the bread, stirring until golden. Remove and drain.

This hearty and nourishing soup, combining garbanzo beans and chicken, is an ideal starter for a family supper.

Chicken *and* Bean Soup

SERVES 4

2 tbsp butter
3 scallions, chopped
2 garlic cloves, chopped finely
1 fresh marjoram sprig, chopped finely
5 cups chicken bouillon
12 oz/350 g boned chicken breasts, diced
12 oz/350 g canned garbanzo beans, drained
1 bouquet garni
1 red bell pepper, diced
1 green bell pepper, diced
1 cup small dried pasta shapes, such as macaroni
salt and white pepper
croûtons, to garnish (see page 25)

1 Melt the butter in a large pan. Add the scallions, garlic, fresh marjoram, and the diced chicken, and cook, stirring frequently, over a medium heat for 5 minutes.

2 Add the chicken bouillon, garbanzo beans, and bouquet garni to the pan and season to taste with salt and white pepper.

3 Bring the soup to a boil, reduce the heat, and simmer gently for about 2 hours.

4 Add the diced bell peppers and pasta to the pan, then simmer for a further 20 minutes.

5 Transfer the soup to a warm tureen. To serve, ladle the soup into warmed individual serving bowls and serve immediately, garnished with croûtons.

NUTRITION
Calories *347*; Sugars *2 g*; Protein *28 g*;
Carbohydrate *37 g*; Fat *11 g*; Saturates *4 g*

moderate

5 mins

2 hr 30 mins

🍳 **COOK'S TIP**

If you prefer, you can use dried garbanzo beans. Cover with cold water and set aside to soak for 5–8 hours. Drain and add the beans to the soup, according to the recipe, and allow an additional 30 minutes to 1 hour cooking time.

This delicately flavoured summer soup is surprisingly easy to make, and tastes delicious.

Lemon *and* Chicken Soup

1 Melt the butter in a large pan. Add the shallots, carrots, celery, and chicken and cook over a low heat, stirring occasionally, for 8 minutes.

2 Thinly pare the lemons and blanch the lemon rind in boiling water for 3 minutes. Squeeze the juice from the lemons.

3 Add the lemon rind and juice to the pan, together with the chicken bouillon. Bring slowly to a boil over a low heat and simmer for about 40 minutes, stirring occasionally.

4 Add the spaghetti to the pan and cook for 15 minutes. Season to taste with salt and white pepper and add the cream. Heat through, but do not allow the soup to boil or it will curdle.

5 Pour the soup into a warmed tureen or individual bowls, garnish with the parsley and half slices of lemon, and serve immediately.

SERVES 4

4 tbsp butter
8 shallots, thinly sliced
2 carrots, thinly sliced
2 celery stalks, thinly sliced
8 oz/225 g boned chicken breasts, chopped finely
3 lemons
5 cups chicken bouillon
8 oz/225 g dried spaghetti, broken into small pieces
2/3 cup heavy cream
salt and white pepper

to garnish
fresh parsley sprig
2 lemon slices, halved

NUTRITION
Calories *506*; Sugars *4 g*; Protein *19 g*; Carbohydrate *41 g*; Fat *31 g*; Saturates *19 g*

 moderate

 5–10 mins

1 hr 15 mins

COOK'S TIP

You can prepare this soup up to the end of step 3 in advance, so that all you need do before serving is heat it through before adding the pasta and the finishing touches.

This aromatic dish originates from Hungary, where goulash soups are often served with dumplings. Noodles are a tasty and quick alternative.

Beef Goulash Soup

SERVES 6

1 tbsp oil

1 lb 2 oz/500 g lean ground beef

2 onions, chopped finely

2 garlic cloves, chopped finely

2 tbsp all-purpose flour

1 cup water

14 oz/400 g canned chopped tomatoes in juice

1 carrot, chopped finely

8 oz/225 g red bell pepper, roasted, peeled, seeded, and chopped

1 tsp Hungarian paprika

1/4 tsp caraway seeds

pinch of dried oregano

4 cups beef bouillon

2 oz/60 g noodles, broken into small pieces

salt and pepper

sour cream and fresh cilantro, to garnish

1 Heat the oil in a large wide pan over a medium-high heat. Add the beef and sprinkle with salt and pepper. Cook until lightly browned.

2 Reduce the heat and add the onions and garlic. Cook for about 3 minutes, stirring frequently, until the onions are softened. Stir in the flour and continue cooking for 1 minute.

3 Add the water and stir to combine well, scraping the bottom of the pan to mix in the flour. Stir in the tomatoes, carrot, pepper, paprika, caraway seeds, oregano, and bouillon.

4 Bring just to a boil. Reduce the heat, cover, and simmer gently for about 40 minutes, stirring occasionally, until all the vegetables are tender.

5 Add the noodles to the soup and simmer for a further 20 minutes or until the noodles are cooked.

6 Taste the soup and adjust the seasoning, if necessary. Ladle into warmed bowls and top each with a tablespoonful of sour cream. Garnish with the fresh cilantro.

NUTRITION

Calories *320*; Sugars *10 g*; Protein *27 g*; Carbohydrate *27 g*; Fat *13 g*; Saturates *5 g*

 easy

15 mins

 1 hr 15 mins

This soup is full of interesting flavors. Chorizo gives it appealing spicy undertones that marry well with the meaty squid.

Squid, Chorizo, *and* Tomato Soup

1 Cut off the squid tentacles and cut into bite-sized pieces. Slice the bodies into rings.

2 Place a large pan over a medium-low heat and add the chorizo. Cook for 5–10 minutes, stirring frequently, until it renders most of its fat. Remove with a slotted spoon and drain on paper towels.

3 Pour off all the fat from the pan and add the onion, celery, carrot, and garlic. Cover and cook for 3–4 minutes or until the onion is slightly softened.

4 Stir in the tomatoes, fish bouillon, cumin, saffron, bay leaf, and chorizo.

5 Add the squid to the soup. Bring almost to a boil, reduce the heat, cover, and cook gently for 40–45 minutes or until the squid and carrot are tender, stirring occasionally.

6 Taste the soup and stir in a little chili paste for a spicier flavor, if wished. Season with salt and pepper. Ladle into warmed bowls, sprinkle with parsley and serve.

SERVES 6

1 lb /450 g cleaned squid
5 ½ oz/150 g lean chorizo, peeled and diced very finely
1 onion, chopped finely
1 celery stalk, sliced thinly
1 carrot, sliced thinly
2 garlic cloves, chopped finely or crushed
14 oz/400 g canned chopped tomatoes in juice
5 cups fish bouillon
½ tsp ground cumin
pinch of saffron
1 bay leaf
salt and pepper
chili paste (optional)
chopped fresh parsley, to garnish

NUTRITION
Calories *165*; Sugars *5 g*; Protein *18 g*; Carbohydrate *7 g*; Fat *8 g*; Saturates *3 g*

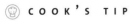 moderate

15 mins

1 hr

COOK'S TIP

Chorizo varies in the amount of fat and the degree of spiciness. A lean style is best for this soup.

This is a really hearty soup, filled with color, flavor, and goodness, which may be adapted to any vegetables that you have at hand.

Mixed Bean Soup

SERVES 4

1 tbsp vegetable oil
1 red onion, halved and sliced
3½ oz/100 g potato, diced
1 carrot, diced
1 leek, sliced
1 fresh green chile, sliced
3 garlic cloves, crushed
1 tsp ground coriander
1 tsp chili powder
4 cups vegetable bouillon
1 lb/450 g mixed canned beans, such as red kidney, borlotti, or small cannellini, drained and rinsed
salt and pepper
2 tbsp chopped fresh cilantro, to garnish

1 Heat the oil in a large pan and add the onion, potato, carrot, and leek. Cook, stirring occasionally, for about 2 minutes or until the vegetables are slightly softened.

2 Add the fresh green chile and garlic and cook for 1 further minute.

3 Stir in the ground coriander, chili powder, and the vegetable bouillon.

4 Bring the soup to a boil, reduce the heat, and cook for 20 minutes or until the vegetables are tender.

5 Stir in the beans, season to taste, and cook, stirring occasionally, for a further 10 minutes.

6 Ladle the soup into warmed bowls, garnish with chopped cilantro, and serve.

NUTRITION
Calories 190; Sugars 9 g; Protein 10 g; Carbohydrate 30 g; Fat 4 g; Saturates 0.5 g

 very easy
5 mins
40 mins

🧑‍🍳 COOK'S TIP
Serve this soup with slices of warm corn bread or a cheese loaf.

This wonderful combination of vegetables, vermicelli, and cannellini beans is made even richer by the addition of pesto and dried mushrooms.

Vegetable *and* Bean Soup

1 Slice the eggplant into rings about ½ inch/1 cm thick, then cut each ring into 4.

2 Cut the tomatoes and potato into small dice. Cut the carrot into sticks about 1 inch/2.5 cm long, and cut the leek into rings.

3 Place the cannellini beans and their liquid in a large pan. Add the eggplant, tomatoes, potatoes, carrot, and leek, stirring to mix.

4 Add the bouillon to the pan and bring to a boil. Reduce the heat and leave to simmer for 15 minutes.

5 Add the basil, dried mushrooms, and their soaking liquid and the vermicelli and simmer for 5 minutes or until all of the vegetables are tender.

6 Remove the pan from the heat and stir in the pesto.

7 Serve with freshly grated Parmesan cheese, if using.

SERVES 4

1 small eggplant
2 large tomatoes
1 potato, peeled
1 carrot, peeled
1 leek
15 oz/425 g canned cannellini beans
3 ¾ cups hot vegetable or chicken bouillon
2 tsp dried basil
½ oz/15 g dried porcini mushrooms, soaked for 10 minutes in enough warm water to cover
¼ cup vermicelli
3 tbsp pesto (see page 77 or use store-bought)
freshly grated Parmesan cheese, to serve (optional)

NUTRITION
Calories *294*; Sugars *2 g*; Protein *11 g*; Carbohydrate *30 g*; Fat *16 g*; Saturates *2 g*

  easy

  30 mins

30 mins

A thick vegetable soup which is a delicious meal in itself. Serve with Parmesan cheese and warm sun-dried tomato bread.

Garbanzo *and* Tomato Soup

SERVES 4

2 tbsp olive oil
2 leeks, sliced
2 zucchini, diced
2 garlic cloves, crushed
4 cups canned chopped tomatoes
1 tbsp tomato paste
1 fresh bay leaf
3½ cups vegetable bouillon
14 oz/400 g canned garbanzo beans, drained and rinsed
8 oz/225 g spinach
salt and pepper

to serve
freshly-grated Parmesan cheese
sun-dried tomato bread

1 Heat the oil in a large pan, then add the leeks and zucchini and cook them briskly for 5 minutes, stirring constantly.

2 Add the garlic, tomatoes, tomato paste, bay leaf, vegetable bouillon, and garbanzo beans.

3 Bring the soup to a boil and simmer for 5 minutes.

4 Shred the spinach finely, add to the soup, and cook for 2 minutes. Season to taste with salt and pepper.

5 Discard the bay leaf. Serve the soup immediately with freshly grated Parmesan cheese and warm sun-dried tomato bread.

NUTRITION
Calories *297*; Sugars *0 g*; Protein *11 g*;
Carbohydrate *24 g*; Fat *18 g*; Saturates *2 g*

 very easy

5 mins

 15 mins

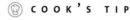 **COOK'S TIP**

Garbanzo beans are used extensively in North African cuisine and are also found in Spanish, Middle Eastern, and Indian cooking. They have a nutty flavor with a firm texture and are excellent canned.

Beans feature widely in Italian soups, making them hearty and tasty. They need to be soaked overnight, so prepare well in advance.

Red Bean Soup

1 Drain the beans and place them in a pan with enough water to cover. Bring to a boil, then boil for 15 minutes to remove any harmful toxins. Reduce the heat and simmer for 45 minutes.

2 Drain the beans and put into a clean pan with the water, ham bone or knuckle, carrots, onion, celery, leek, bay leaves, and olive oil. Bring to a boil, then cover, and simmer for 1 hour or until the beans are very tender.

3 Discard the bay leaves and bone, reserving any ham pieces from the bone. Remove a small cupful of the beans and reserve. Purée or blend the soup in a food processor or blender, or push through a coarse strainer, and return to a clean pan.

4 Add the tomatoes, garlic, tomato paste, rice, and seasoning. Bring back to a boil and simmer for about 15 minutes or until the rice is tender.

5 Add the cabbage and reserved beans and ham, and continue to simmer for 5 minutes. Adjust the seasoning and serve very hot. If liked, a piece of toasted crusty bread may be put in the base of each soup bowl before ladling in the soup. If the soup is too thick, add a little boiling water or bouillon.

SERVES 4

scant 1 cup dried red kidney beans, soaked overnight
7½ cups water
1 large ham bone or bacon knuckle
2 carrots, chopped
1 large onion, chopped
2 celery stalks, sliced thinly
1 leek, trimmed, washed, and sliced
1–2 bay leaves
2 tbsp olive oil
2–3 tomatoes, peeled and chopped
1 garlic clove, crushed
1 tbsp tomato paste
4½ tbsp arborio or Italian rice
4–6 oz/125–175 g green cabbage, shredded finely
salt and pepper

NUTRITION
Calories *184*; Sugars *5 g*; Protein *4 g*; Carbohydrate *19 g*; Fat *11 g*; Saturates *2 g*

easy

5–10 mins

3 hrs

In Italy, this soup is called Minestrade Lentiche. A Minestra is a soup cooked with pasta; here, farfalline, a small bow-shaped variety, is used.

Brown Lentil *and* Pasta Soup

SERVES 4

4 rashers lean bacon, cut into small squares
1 onion, chopped
2 garlic cloves, crushed
2 celery stalks, chopped
¼ cup farfalline or spaghetti, broken into small pieces
14 oz/400 g canned brown lentils, drained
5 cups hot ham or vegetable bouillon
2 tbsp chopped, fresh mint

1 Place the bacon in a large skillet together with the onions, garlic, and celery. Dry fry for 4–5 minutes, stirring, until the onion is tender and the bacon is just beginning to brown.

2 Add the pasta to the skillet and cook, stirring, for about 1 minute to coat the pasta in the oil.

3 Add the lentils and the bouillon and bring to a boil. Reduce the heat and leave to simmer for 12–15 minutes or until the pasta is tender.

4 Remove the skillet from the heat and stir in the chopped fresh mint.

5 Transfer the soup to warmed soup bowls and serve immediately.

NUTRITION

Calories *225*; Sugars *1 g*; Protein *13 g*;
Carbohydrate *27 g*; Fat *8 g*; Saturates *3 g*

 very easy

🕐 5 mins

🕐 25 mins

🍳 COOK'S TIP

If you prefer to use dried lentils, add the bouillon before the pasta and cook for 1–1¼ hours or until the lentils are tender. Add the pasta and cook for a further 12–15 minutes.

Minestrone translates as "big soup" in Italian. It is made all over Italy, but this version comes from Livorno, a port on the western coast.

Minestrone

1 Heat the olive oil in a large pan. Add the diced pancetta, chopped onions, and garlic and cook for about 5 minutes, stirring, or until the onions are soft and golden.

2 Add the prepared potato, carrot, leek, cabbage, and celery to the pan. Cook for a further 2 minutes, stirring frequently, to coat all of the vegetables in the oil.

3 Add the tomatoes, small navy beans, hot ham or chicken bouillon, and bouquet garni to the pan, stirring to mix. Leave the soup to simmer, covered, for 15–20 minutes or until all of the vegetables are just tender.

4 Remove the bouquet garni, season with salt and pepper to taste, and serve with plenty of freshly grated Parmesan cheese.

SERVES 4

1 tbsp olive oil
3½ oz/100 g pancetta ham, diced
2 medium onions, chopped
2 cloves garlic, crushed
1 potato, peeled and cut into
    ½-inch/1-cm cubes
1 carrot, peeled and cut into chunks
1 leek, sliced into rings
¼ green cabbage, shredded
1 celery stalk, chopped
1 lb/450 g canned chopped tomatoes
7 oz/200 g canned small navy beans, drained
    and rinsed
2½ cups hot ham or chicken bouillon,
    diluted with 2½ cups boiling water
bouquet garni (2 bay leaves, 2 sprigs thyme,
    and 2 sprigs rosemary, tied together)
salt and pepper
freshly grated Parmesan cheese, to serve

NUTRITION
Calories 311; Sugars 8 g; Protein 12 g;
Carbohydrate 26 g; Fat 19 g; Saturates 5 g

 very easy

10 mins

 30 mins

This classic soup is very popular throughout the world. When pumpkin is out of season, use butternut squash in its place.

Pumpkin Soup

SERVES 6

about 2 lb/900 g pumpkin
3 tbsp butter or margarine
1 onion, sliced thinly
1 garlic clove, crushed
3½ cups vegetable bouillon
½ tsp ground ginger
1 tbsp lemon juice
3–4 thinly pared strips of orange zest (optional)
1–2 bay leaves or 1 bouquet garni
1¼ cups milk
salt and pepper

to garnish
4–6 tbsp light or heavy cream or plain yogurt
snipped chives

1 Peel the pumpkin, remove the seeds, and then cut the flesh into 1-inch/ 2.5-cm cubes.

2 Melt the butter or margarine in a large, heavy pan. Add the onion and garlic and cook over low heat until soft, but not colored.

3 Add the pumpkin and toss with the onion for 2–3 minutes.

4 Add the bouillon and bring to a boil over medium heat. Season to taste with salt and pepper and add the ground ginger and lemon juice, the strips of orange zest, if using, and the bay leaves or bouquet garni.

5 Cover the pan and gently simmer the soup over low heat for about 20 minutes, stirring occasionally, until the pumpkin is tender.

6 Discard the orange zest, if using, and the bay leaves or bouquet garni. Cool the soup slightly, then press through a strainer with the back of a spoon, or process in a food processor until smooth. Pour into a clean pan.

7 Add the milk and reheat gently. Adjust the seasoning. Garnish with a swirl of cream or plain yogurt and snipped chives, and serve.

NUTRITION
Calories *112*; Sugars *7 g*; Protein *4 g*;
Carbohydrate *8 g*; Fat *7 g*; Saturates *2 g*

           very easy

10 mins

30 mins

Sweet red bell peppers and tangy tomatoes are blended together in a smooth vegetable soup that makes a perfect starter or light lunch.

Tomato *and* Red Bell Pepper Soup

1 Preheat the broiler to hot. Halve and deseed the bell peppers, arrange them on the broiler rack and cook, turning occasionally, for 8–10 minutes or until softened and charred.

2 Leave to cool slightly, then carefully peel off the charred skin. Reserving a small piece for garnish, chop the bell pepper flesh and place in a large pan.

3 Mix in the onion, celery, and garlic. Add the bouillon and the bay leaves. Bring to a boil, cover, and simmer for 15 minutes. Remove from the heat.

4 Stir in the tomatoes and transfer to a blender. Process for a few seconds until smooth. Return to the pan.

5 Season to taste and heat for 3–4 minutes or until piping hot. Ladle into warmed bowls and garnish with the reserved bell pepper cut into strips and the scallion floating on the top. Serve with crusty bread.

SERVES 4

2 large red bell peppers
1 large onion, chopped
2 celery stalks, trimmed and chopped
1 garlic clove, crushed
2½ cups fresh vegetable bouillon
2 bay leaves
28 oz/800 g canned plum tomatoes
salt and pepper
2 scallions, shredded finely, to garnish
crusty bread, to serve

NUTRITION
Calories *147*; Sugars *28 g*; Protein *3 g*; Carbohydrate *29 g*; Fat *0.4 g*; Saturates *0 g*

 moderate

 45 mins

 25 mins

COOK'S TIP

If you prefer a coarser, more robust soup, lightly mash the tomatoes with a wooden spoon and omit the blending process in step 4.

This delicately flavored apple and apricot soup is gently spiced with ginger and allspice and finished with a swirl of sour cream.

Spiced Fruit Soup

SERVES 4

generous 1 cup dried apricots, soaked overnight, or no-soak dried apricots

1 lb 2 oz/500 g eating apples, peeled, cored, and chopped

1 small onion, chopped

1 tbsp lemon or lime juice

3 cups vegetable bouillon

²/₃ cup dry white wine

¼ tsp ground ginger

pinch of ground allspice

salt and pepper

to garnish

4–6 tbsp sour cream

ground ginger or allspice

1 Drain the apricots, if necessary, and chop coarsely.

2 Put the apricots in a pan and add the apples, onion, lemon or lime juice, and bouillon. Bring to a boil, cover, and simmer gently for about 20 minutes.

3 Set the soup aside to cool a little, then press through a strainer or process in a food processor or blender until a smooth purée. Pour the fruit soup into a clean pan.

4 Add the wine and spices to the soup and season to taste.

5 Bring back to a boil, then let cool. If the soup is too thick, add a little more bouillon or water. Transfer to a serving bowl and chill in the refrigerator for several hours.

6 To serve, garnish with sour cream and dust lightly with ginger or allspice.

NUTRITION

Calories 147; Sugars 28 g; Protein 3 g; Carbohydrate 29 g; Fat 0.4 g; Saturates 0 g

easy

7 hrs 45 mins

25 mins

 COOK'S TIP

Other fruits can be combined with apples to make fruit soups—try raspberries, blackberries, black currants, or cherries. If the fruits have a lot of seeds or pits, the soup should be strained after puréeing.

Spinach is the basis for this delicious soup, which has creamy mascarpone cheese stirred through it to give it a wonderful texture.

Spinach *and* Mascarpone Soup

1 Melt half the butter in a very large pan. Add the scallions and celery, and cook them over medium heat, stirring frequently, for about 5 minutes or until soft.

2 Pack the spinach, sorrel, or watercress into the pan. Add the vegetable bouillon and bring to a boil, then reduce the heat, cover, and simmer for about 15–20 minutes.

3 Transfer the soup to a blender or food processor and process until smooth. Alternatively, rub it through a strainer. Return to the pan.

4 Add the mascarpone to the soup and heat gently, stirring constantly, until smooth and blended. Season to taste with salt and pepper.

5 Heat the remaining butter with the olive oil in a skillet. Add the bread cubes and cook, turning frequently, until golden brown, adding the caraway seeds toward the end of cooking, so that they do not burn.

6 Ladle the soup into warmed bowls. Sprinkle with the croûtons and serve with the sesame bread sticks.

SERVES 4

4 tbsp butter
1 bunch scallions, trimmed and chopped
2 celery stalks, chopped
3/4 lb/350 g spinach or sorrel, or 3 bunches watercress
3½ cups vegetable bouillon
8 oz/225 g mascarpone cheese
1 tbsp olive oil
2 slices thick-cut bread, cut into cubes
½ tsp caraway seeds
salt and pepper
sesame bread sticks, to serve

NUTRITION
Calories *402*; Sugars *2 g*; Protein *11 g*; Carbohydrate *10 g*; Fat *36 g*; Saturates *21 g*

 very easy

15 mins

 30 mins

🍲 COOK'S TIP

Any leafy vegetable can be used to vary the flavor of this soup. For anyone who grows their own vegetables, it is the perfect recipe for experimenting with a glut of produce. Try young beet greens or surplus lettuces for a change.

International Soups

Today people travel the world as a matter of course, and as we have access to more culinary influences our tastes have become more demanding. This chapter caters for that desire for unusual recipes by featuring an international range of modern-day soups, incorporating unusual ingredients such as sweet potato and arugula with flavorings such as curry and dill. Recipes have been drawn from Senegal, Eastern Europe, the Americas, and the Caribbean; there is something for the most discerning of palates to enjoy.

When there's a chill in the air, this vivid soup is just the thing to serve—it's very warm and comforting.

Sweet Potato Soup

SERVES 6

¾ lb/350 g sweet potatoes
1 acorn squash
4 shallots
olive oil
5–6 garlic cloves, unpeeled
3¾ cups vegetable bouillon
½ cup light cream
salt and pepper
snipped chives, to garnish

1 Cut the sweet potato, squash, and shallots in half lengthwise. Brush the cut sides with oil.

2 Put the vegetables, cut sides down, in a shallow roasting pan. Add the garlic cloves. Roast in a preheated oven, 375°F/190°C for about 40 minutes or until tender and light brown.

3 When cool, scoop the flesh from the potato and squash halves and put in a pan with the shallots. Remove the garlic peel and add the soft insides to the other vegetables.

4 Add the bouillon and a pinch of salt. Bring just to a boil, then reduce the heat, and simmer, partially covered, for about 30 minutes, stirring occasionally, until the vegetables are very tender.

5 Let the soup cool slightly, then transfer to a blender or food processor and purée until smooth, working in batches, if necessary. (If using a food processor, strain off the cooking liquid and reserve. Purée the soup solids with enough cooking liquid to moisten them, then combine with the remaining liquid.)

6 Return the soup to the pan and stir in the cream. Season to taste, then simmer for 5–10 minutes or until completely heated through. Ladle into warmed bowls and serve hot garnished with chives.

NUTRITION
Calories 57; Sugars 1.5 g; Protein 2.3 g;
Carbohydrate 6.6 g; Fat 2.5 g; Saturates 1 g

 moderate

 15 mins

15 mins

1 hr 15 mins

A dried ancho chili adds a kick to this glowing Mexican corn soup. The corn kernels are tossed in butter, giving the soup a roasted flavor.

Corn Soup *with* Chilis

1 Put the chili in a bowl and cover with boiling water. Let stand for about 15 minutes to soften.

2 Melt the butter in a skillet over medium-low heat. Add the corn and turn to coat. Cook for about 15 minutes, stirring frequently, until it starts to brown slightly. Add the onion, garlic, and bell pepper and cook for about 7–10 minutes, stirring frequently, until the onion is soft and the mixture starts to stick.

3 Transfer the mixture to a blender or food processor, add the bouillon or water, and purée until smooth.

4 Put the cream in a large pan, stir in the puréed vegetables, and bring almost to a boil. Add the cumin. Season with a little salt. Adjust the heat so the soup bubbles very gently and continue to cook until the mixture is reduced by about one-quarter.

5 Remove the ancho chili from its liquid and discard the core and the seeds. (Wash your hands well after preparing chilis, as they can irritate the skin.) Put the chili into a blender or food processor with 4–5 tablespoons of the soaking water and purée until smooth.

6 Stir 2–4 tablespoons of the purée into the soup, according to taste, and continue cooking for a further 5 minutes.

7 Taste the soup and adjust the seasoning, if necessary. Ladle the soup into warmed bowls, garnish with cilantro or parsley, and serve.

SERVES 4

1 dried ancho chili
4 tbsp butter
3½ cups defrosted frozen corn kernels
1 large onion, chopped finely
1 large garlic clove, chopped finely
1 red bell pepper, cored, seeded, and finely chopped
1¼ cups vegetable bouillon or water
2½ cups whipping cream
½ tsp ground cumin
salt
chopped fresh cilantro or parsley, to garnish

NUTRITION
Calories *824*; Sugars *12 g*; Protein *9 g*; Carbohydrate *33 g*; Fat *74 g*; Saturates *45 g*

 moderate

25 mins

35 mins

Glass bowls are pretty for serving this soup, which makes a very light and refreshing appetizer for warm days.

Melon Gazpacho

SERVES 4

1 tsp oil
1 onion, chopped finely
1 large garlic clove, chopped finely
1 tsp chopped fresh chile
1 lb 9 oz/700 g seedless Cantaloupe melon
    flesh, cubed
½ tsp raspberry vinegar or 1 tsp lemon juice
½ ripe green melon, about 1 lb 2 oz/500 g
salt
chopped chives, to garnish

1 Heat the oil in a small pan over low heat. Add the onion, garlic, and chile and cook, stirring occasionally, for about 6–7 minutes or until the onion is softened, but not browned.

2 Put the Cantaloupe melon flesh in a blender or food processor, add the onion, garlic, and chile, and process to a smooth purée, stopping to scrape down the sides as needed. You may need to work in batches. Add the vinegar or lemon juice with a pinch of salt and process briefly to combine.

3 Cover with plastic wrap and chill in the refrigerator for about 30 minutes or until the mixture is cold.

4 Remove the seeds from the green melon, then cut into balls with a melon baller. Alternatively, cut into cubes with a sharp knife.

5 Divide the soup equally among four shallow bowls and then top each one with some green melon balls. Sprinkle lightly with chopped fresh chives to garnish and then serve.

NUTRITION
Calories *98*; Sugars *20 g*; Protein *3 g*;
Carbohydrate *21 g*; Fat *1 g*; Saturates *0 g*

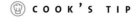

easy

45 mins

6–7 mins

 COOK'S TIP

If you are wary of using fresh chile, omit it and add a few drops of hot pepper sauce to taste at the end of Step 2 to liven up the soup.

This soup is made from raw vegetables and fruit, so it is full of goodness, as well as flavor, and is wonderfully refreshing on a warm day.

Cold Tomato *and* Orange Soup

1 Working over a bowl to catch the juices, peel the oranges. Cut down between the membranes and drop the orange segments into the bowl.

2 Put the tomatoes in a small bowl and pour over boiling water to cover. Stand for 10 seconds, then drain. Peel off the skins and cut the tomatoes in half crosswise. Scoop out the seeds into a strainer set over a bowl; reserve the tomato juices.

3 Put the tomatoes, celery, and carrots in a blender or food processor. Add the orange segments and their juice and the juice saved from the tomatoes. Process to a smooth purée.

4 Scrape into a bowl and stir in the tomato juice. Cover with plastic wrap and chill until cold.

5 Taste the soup and add salt, if needed, and a few drops of Tabasco sauce, if wished. Stir in the chopped mint, ladle into cold bowls, and garnish with fresh mint sprigs.

SERVES 4

3 large seedless oranges
4 ripe tomatoes
2 celery stalks, chopped
3 carrots, grated
1½ cups tomato juice
salt
Tabasco sauce (optional)
1 tbsp chopped fresh mint
fresh mint sprigs, to garnish

NUTRITION
Calories *98*; Sugars *22 g*; Protein *3 g*; Carbohydrate *22 g*; Fat *0 g*; Saturates *0 g*

easy
45 mins
0 mins

COOK'S TIP

This soup really needs to be made in a blender for the best texture. A food processor can be used, but the soup will not be completely smooth.

There are innumerable versions of this soup of Eastern European origin. This refreshing vegetarian version is light and full of flavor.

Chilled Borscht

SERVES 4

¼ medium cabbage, cored and coarsely chopped
1 tbsp vegetable oil
1 onion, chopped finely
1 leek, halved lengthwise and sliced
14 oz/400 g canned peeled tomatoes
5 cups water, plus extra if needed
1 carrot, sliced thinly
1 small parsnip, chopped finely
3 beets (raw or cooked), peeled and cubed
1 bay leaf
1½ cups tomato juice
2–3 tbsp chopped fresh dill
fresh lemon juice (optional)
salt and pepper
sour cream or plain yogurt, to garnish

NUTRITION
Calories 93; Sugars 12 g; Protein 4 g;
Carbohydrate 15 g; Fat 3 g; Saturates 0 g

moderate

45 mins

1 hr 30 mins

1 Cover the cabbage generously with cold water in a pan. Bring to a boil, cook for 3 minutes, then drain.

2 Heat the oil in a large pan over medium-low heat. Add the onion and leek, cover, and cook, stirring occasionally, for about 5 minutes or until the vegetables begin to soften.

3 Add the tomatoes, water, carrot, parsnip, beets, and bay leaf. Stir in the blanched cabbage and add a pinch of salt. Bring to a boil, reduce the heat, and simmer for about 1¼ hours or until all the vegetables are tender. Remove and discard the bay leaf.

4 Remove the pan from the heat and set aside to cool slightly, then transfer to a blender or food processor, and process to a smooth purée, working in batches if necessary. (If using a food processor, strain off the cooking liquid and reserve. Purée the soup solids with enough cooking liquid to moisten them, then combine with the remaining liquid.)

5 Scrape the soup into a large container and stir in the tomato juice. Set aside to cool, then chill in the refrigerator.

6 Stir in the dill. Thin the soup with more tomato juice or water, if wished. Season to taste with salt and pepper and lemon juice, if wished. Ladle into chilled soup bowls, top each with a spiral of sour cream or a spoon of yogurt.

A chunky mix of colorful vegetables, highlighted with Mexican flavors, this cold soup makes a lively appetizer at the start of any meal.

Iced Salsa Soup

1 Cut the corn kernels from the cobs, or if using frozen corn, thaw and drain.

2 Heat the oil in a pan over medium-high heat. Add the bell peppers and cook, stirring briskly, for 3 minutes. Add the onion and continue cooking for about 2 minutes or until it starts to color slightly.

3 Add the tomatoes, corn, and chili powder. Continue cooking, stirring frequently, for 1 minute. Pour in the water and when it begins to boil, reduce the heat, cover, and cook for a further 4–5 minutes or until the bell peppers are just barely tender.

4 Transfer the mixture to a large container and stir in the tomato juice. Season with salt and pepper to taste and add more chili powder if wished. Cover with plastic wrap and chill in the refrigerator until cold.

5 Taste and adjust the seasoning. For a spicier soup, stir in a little chili paste to taste. For a thinner soup, add a small amount of ice water. Ladle into chilled bowls and garnish with scallions and fresh cilantro leaves.

SERVES 4

2 large corn cobs or 1⅓ cups frozen corn kernels
1 tbsp olive oil
1 orange or red bell pepper, seeded and finely chopped
1 green bell pepper, seeded and finely chopped
1 sweet onion, such as Vidalia, chopped finely
3 ripe tomatoes, peeled, seeded, and chopped
½ tsp chili powder
½ cup water
2 cups tomato juice
chili paste (optional)
salt and pepper

to garnish
3–4 scallions, chopped finely
fresh cilantro leaves

NUTRITION
Calories *138*; Sugars *12 g*; Protein *5 g*; Carbohydrate *22 g*; Fat *4 g*; Saturates *1 g*

⭐⭐ easy
 45 mins
 12–15 mins

This simple recipe uses the sweet potato with its distinctive flavor and color, combined with a hint of orange and cilantro.

Sweet Potato *and* Onion Soup

SERVES 4

2 tbsp vegetable oil
2 lb/900 g sweet potatoes, diced
1 carrot, diced
2 onions, sliced
2 garlic cloves, crushed
2½ cups vegetable bouillon
1¼ cups unsweetened orange juice
1 cup lowfat plain yogurt
2 tbsp chopped fresh cilantro
salt and pepper

to garnish
fresh cilantro sprigs
orange zest

1 Heat the vegetable oil in a large, heavy pan and add the sweet potatoes, carrot, onions, and garlic. Cook the vegetables over low heat, stirring constantly for 5 minutes until soft.

2 Pour in the vegetable bouillon and orange juice and bring to a boil.

3 Reduce the heat to a simmer, cover the pan, and cook the vegetables for 20 minutes or until the sweet potatoes and carrot are tender.

4 Transfer the mixture to a food processor or blender, in batches, and process for 1 minute or until puréed. Return the purée to the rinsed-out pan.

5 Stir in the yogurt and chopped cilantro and season to taste with salt and pepper.

6 Serve the soup in warmed bowls and garnish with fresh cilantro sprigs and orange zest.

NUTRITION
Calories *320*; Sugars *26 g*; Protein *7 g*;
Carbohydrate *62 g*; Fat *7 g*; Saturates *1 g*

 very easy

15 mins

30 mins

 COOK'S TIP

This soup can be chilled before serving, if preferred. If chilling, stir the yogurt into the dish just before serving. Serve in chilled bowls.

This hearty soup is wonderful made in the middle of winter with fresh seasonal vegetables. Use a really well-flavored sharp colby cheese.

Cheesy Vegetable Chowder

1 Melt the butter in a large, heavy pan over medium-low heat. Add the onion, leek, and garlic. Cover and cook for about 5 minutes, stirring frequently, until the vegetables start to soften.

2 Stir the flour into the vegetables and continue cooking for 2 minutes. Add a little of the bouillon and stir well, scraping the bottom of the pan to mix in the flour. Bring to a boil, stirring frequently, and slowly stir in the rest of the bouillon.

3 Add the carrots, celery, turnip, potato, thyme, and bay leaf. Reduce the heat, cover, and cook gently for about 35 minutes, stirring occasionally, until the vegetables are tender. Remove the bay leaf and the thyme sprigs.

4 Stir the light cream into the soup and simmer over very low heat for 5 minutes. Add the grated cheese a handful at a time, stirring constantly for 1 minute after each addition, to make sure it is completely melted.

5 Taste the soup and adjust the seasoning, adding salt if needed, and pepper to taste.

6 Serve immediately in warmed bowls, garnished with fresh chopped parsley.

SERVES 4

2 tbsp butter
1 large onion, finely chopped
1 large leek, split lengthwise and thinly sliced
1–2 garlic cloves, crushed
6 tbsp all-purpose flour
5 cups vegetable bouillon
3 carrots, finely diced
2 celery stalks, finely diced
1 turnip, finely diced
1 large potato, finely diced
3–4 sprigs fresh thyme, or 1/8 tsp dried thyme
1 bay leaf
1 1/2 cups light cream
2 1/4 cups grated sharp colby cheese
chopped fresh parsley, to garnish
salt and pepper

NUTRITION
Calories *669*; Sugars *13 g*; Protein *26 g*; Carbohydrate *33 g*; Fat *49 g*; Saturates *30 g*

  moderate

15 mins

50 mins

Arugula has a distinctive flavor that blends well with lettuce in this delicious creamy soup. The rice adds body to the soup.

Lettuce *and* Arugula Soup

SERVES 4

1 tbsp butter
1 large sweet onion, halved and sliced
2 leeks, sliced
6¼ cups vegetable bouillon
6 tbsp white rice
2 carrots, sliced thinly
3 garlic cloves
1 bay leaf
2 heads soft round lettuce (about 1 lb/ 450 g), cored and chopped
¾ cup heavy cream
freshly grated nutmeg
3 oz/85 g arugula leaves, chopped finely
salt and pepper
arugula leaves, to garnish

NUTRITION
Calories *253*; Sugars *8 g*; Protein *4 g*;
Carbohydrate *21 g*; Fat *18 g*; Saturates *10 g*

 moderate

15 mins

55 mins

1 Heat the butter in a large pan over medium heat and add the onion and leeks. Cover and cook for 3–4 minutes, stirring frequently, until the vegetables begin to soften.

2 Add the bouillon, rice, carrots, garlic, and bay leaf with a large pinch of salt. Bring just to a boil. Reduce the heat, cover, and simmer for 25–30 minutes or until the rice and vegetables are tender. Remove the bay leaf.

3 Add the chopped lettuce and cook for 10 minutes or until the leaves are soft, stirring occasionally.

4 Let the soup cool slightly, then transfer to a blender or food processor and purée until smooth, working in batches if necessary. (If using a food processor, strain off the cooking liquid and reserve. Purée the soup solids with enough cooking liquid to moisten them, then combine with the remaining liquid.)

5 Return the soup to the pan and place over medium-low heat. Stir in the cream and a grating of nutmeg. Simmer gently for about 5 minutes, stirring occasionally, until the soup is reheated. Add more water or cream if you prefer a thinner soup.

6 Add the arugula and simmer for 2–3 minutes, stirring occasionally, until it is wilted. Adjust the seasoning, ladle the soup into warmed bowls, and garnish with arugula leaves.

This soup uses canned tuna and tomatoes, two pantry favorites that you are likely to have on hand, for a quickly made lunch or supper.

Curried Tuna Chowder

1 Drain the tuna over a measuring cup and add boiling water to make the liquid up to 2½ cups.

2 Melt the butter in a large pan over a medium-low heat. Add the chopped onion and garlic and cook for about 5 minutes or until the onion is softened, stirring frequently.

3 Stir in the flour and curry powder. Continue cooking for 2 minutes.

4 Slowly add about half of the tuna juice and water mixture and stir well, scraping the bottom of the pan to mix in the flour. Pour in the remaining mixture and bring just to a boil, stirring frequently. Add the tomatoes and break up with a spoon. When the soup almost comes back to a boil, stir in the rice, reduce the heat, cover, and simmer for about 10 minutes.

5 Add the tuna and zucchini to the soup and continue cooking for about 15 minutes or until the vegetables and rice are tender.

6 Stir in the cream, season with salt and pepper to taste, and continue simmering for about 3–4 minutes until heated through. Ladle the soup into warmed bowls and serve.

SERVES 4

7 oz/200 g canned light meat tuna packed in water
1½ tbsp butter
1 onion, chopped finely
1 garlic clove, chopped finely
2 tbsp all-purpose flour
2 tsp mild curry powder
14 oz/400 g canned plum tomatoes in juice
3 tbsp white rice
1 zucchini, diced finely
½ cup light cream
salt and pepper

NUTRITION
Calories 239; Sugars 5 g; Protein 16 g; Carbohydrate 20 g; Fat 11 g; Saturates 7 g

★★★ moderate
 5–10 mins
 40–50 mins

Mussels, an economical choice at the fish store, give essential flavor to this soup. The proportions of fish and shrimp are flexible.

Seafood Chowder

SERVES 6

2 lb 4 oz/1 kg mussels
4 tbsp all-purpose flour
6¼ cups fish bouillon
1 tbsp butter
1 large onion, chopped finely
12 oz/350 g skinless white fish fillets, such as cod, sole, or haddock
7 oz/200 g cooked or raw peeled shrimp
1¼ cups whipping cream or heavy cream
salt and pepper
snipped fresh dill, to garnish

NUTRITION
Calories *449*; Sugars *4 g*; Protein *34 g*;
Carbohydrate *18 g*; Fat *27 g*; Saturates *16 g*

⭐⭐⭐   moderate

    30 mins

🕐   40 mins

1 Discard any broken mussels and those with open shells. Rinse, pull off any "beards" and if there are barnacles, scrape them off with a knife under cold running water. Put the mussels in a large, heavy-based pan. Cover tightly and cook over a high heat for about 4 minutes or until the mussels open, shaking the pan occasionally. Remove the mussels from their shells, adding any juices to the cooking liquid. Strain through a cheesecloth-lined strainer and reserve.

2 Put the flour in a mixing bowl and very slowly whisk in enough of the bouillon to make a thick paste. Whisk in a little more bouillon to make a smooth liquid.

3 Melt the butter in heavy-based pan over a medium-low heat. Add the onion, cover, and cook for about 5 minutes, stirring frequently, until it softens.

4 Add the remaining fish bouillon and bring to a boil. Slowly whisk in the flour mixture until well combined and bring back to a boil, whisking constantly. Add the mussel cooking liquid. Season with salt, if needed, and pepper. Reduce the heat and simmer, partially covered, for 15 minutes.

5 Add the fish and mussels and continue simmering, stirring occasionally, for about 5 minutes or until the fish is cooked and begins to flake.

6 Stir in the shrimp and cream. Taste and then adjust the seasoning. Simmer for a few minutes more to heat through. Ladle into warmed bowls, sprinkle the soup with fresh dill and serve.

This soup is swimming with seafood. Depending on availability, you could substitute skinless, boneless white fish for the scallops or shrimp.

Shellfish *and* Tomato Soup

1 Discard any broken mussels and those with open shells that do not close when tapped. Rinse, pull off any "beards", and if there are barnacles, scrape them off with a knife under cold running water. Put the mussels in a large heavy-based pan, cover tightly and cook for 4–5 minutes or until the mussels open, shaking the pan occasionally.

2 When they are cool enough to handle, remove the mussels from the shells, adding additional juices to the cooking liquid. Strain the liquid through a cheesecloth-lined strainer. Top it up with water to make 2 cups.

3 Melt the butter in a large pan over a medium–low heat. Add the shallots and cook for 3–4 minutes, stirring frequently, until soft. Stir in the flour and continue cooking for 2 minutes. Add the wine.

4 Slowly add the fish bouillon and stir well, scraping the bottom of the pan to mix in the flour. Pour in the remaining mussel cooking liquid and water and bring just to a boil, stirring frequently. Reduce the heat, cover and simmer for 10 minutes.

5 Add the scallops, shrimp, and mussels, and continue cooking for 1 minute.

6 Stir in the cream, tomatoes, chives, and most of the parsley. Season to taste with salt. Sprinkle with the remaining parsley and serve.

SERVES **4**

2 lb 4 oz/1 kg mussels
2 tbsp butter
2 shallots, chopped finely
4 tbsp all-purpose flour
4 tbsp dry white wine
2½ cups fish bouillon
7 oz/200 g bay scallops
7 oz/200 g cooked peeled shrimp
½ cup heavy cream
4 tomatoes, peeled, seeded, and chopped
2 tbsp snipped fresh chives
2 tbsp chopped fresh parsley
salt and pepper

NUTRITION
Calories *316*; Sugars *3 g*; Protein *26 g*;
Carbohydrate *21 g*; Fat *14 g*; Saturates *8 g*

 moderate

15 mins

 35 mins

For this tasty and unusual soup, boneless leg is a good cut of beef to use, as it is generally lean and any fat is easily trimmed off.

Mexican-Style Beef *and* Rice Soup

SERVES 4

3 tbsp olive oil
1 lb 2 oz/500 g boneless stewing beef, cut into 1-inch/2.5-cm pieces
2/3 cup red wine
1 onion, finely chopped
1 green bell pepper, cored, seeded, and finely chopped
1 small fresh red chile, seeded, and finely chopped
2 garlic cloves, chopped finely
1 carrot, chopped finely
1/4 tsp ground coriander
1/4 tsp ground cumin
1/4 tsp dried oregano
1/8 tsp ground cinnamon
1 bay leaf
grated zest of 1/2 orange
14 oz/400 g canned chopped tomatoes
5 cups beef bouillon
1/4 cup long-grain white rice
3 tbsp raisins
1/2 oz/15 g semi-sweet chocolate, melted
chopped fresh cilantro, to garnish

NUTRITION
Calories 501; Sugars 45 g; Protein 14 g;
Carbohydrate 36 g; Fat 18 g; Saturates 5 g

 easy

15 mins

 2 hrs

1 Heat half the oil in a large skillet over a medium-high heat. Add the meat in one layer and cook until well browned, turning to color all sides. Remove the pan from the heat and pour in the wine.

2 Heat the remaining oil in a large pan over a medium heat. Add the onion, cover, and cook for about 3 minutes, stirring occasionally, until just softened. Add the green bell pepper, chile, garlic, and carrot, and continue cooking, covered, for 3 minutes.

3 Add the coriander, cumin, oregano, cinnamon, bay leaf, and orange zest to the pan. Stir in the tomatoes and bouillon, along with the beef and wine. Bring almost to a boil and when the mixture begins to bubble, reduce the heat to low. Cover and simmer gently, stirring occasionally, for about 1 hour or until the meat is tender.

4 Stir in the rice, raisins, and chocolate, and continue cooking, stirring occasionally, for about 30 minutes or until the rice is tender.

5 Ladle into warmed bowls and garnish with cilantro.

Spicy or smoky sausages add substance to this soup, which makes a hearty and warming supper, served with crusty bread and green salad.

Cabbage Soup *with* Sausage

1 Put the sausages in water to cover generously and bring to a boil. Reduce the heat and simmer until firm. Drain the sausages and, when cool enough to handle, remove the skin, if you wish, and slice thinly.

2 Heat the oil in a large pan over a medium heat, add the onion, leek, and carrots and cook for 3–4 minutes, stirring frequently, until the onion starts to soften.

3 Add the tomatoes, cabbage, garlic, thyme, bouillon, and sausages. Bring to a boil, reduce the heat to low, and cook gently, partially covered, for about 40 minutes or until the vegetables are tender.

4 Taste the soup and adjust the seasoning, if necessary. Ladle into warmed bowls and serve with Parmesan cheese.

SERVES 6

12 oz/350 g lean sausages, preferably highly seasoned
2 tsp oil
1 onion, finely chopped
1 leek, halved lengthways and sliced thinly
2 carrots, halved and thinly sliced
14 oz/400 g canned chopped tomatoes
12 oz/350 g young green cabbage, cored and coarsely shredded
1-2 garlic cloves, chopped finely
pinch dried thyme
6¼ cups chicken or meat bouillon
salt and pepper
freshly grated Parmesan cheese, to serve

NUTRITION
Calories *160*; Sugars *10 g*; Protein *7 g*; Carbohydrate *12 g*; Fat *8 g*; Saturates *2 g*

 moderate
10 mins
 1 hr 15 mins

COOK'S TIP

If you don't have fresh bouillon available, use water instead, with 1 bouillon cube only dissolved in it. Add a little more onion and garlic, plus a bouquet garni (remove it before serving).

This soup is perfect for the sweet meat of rabbit, which is traditionally paired with tomatoes and mushrooms.

Hunter's Soup

SERVES 4

1–2 tbsp olive oil
2 lb/900 g rabbit portions
1 onion, finely chopped
2–3 garlic cloves, chopped finely or crushed
generous ½ cup finely chopped lean smoked bacon
½ cup white wine
5 cups chicken bouillon
2 cups tomato juice
2 tbsp tomato paste
2 carrots, halved lengthwise and sliced
1 bay leaf
¼ tsp dried thyme
¼ tsp dried oregano
1 tbsp butter
10½ oz/300 g mushrooms, sliced or quartered if small
salt and pepper
chopped fresh parsley, to garnish

NUTRITION
Calories 377; Sugars 13 g; Protein 36 g; Carbohydrate 16 g; Fat 17 g; Saturates 6 g

 moderate

 20 mins

20 mins

2 hrs 30 mins

1 Heat the oil in a large pan over medium heat. Add the rabbit, in batches if necessary, and cook until lightly browned on all sides, adding a little more oil if needed. Remove from the pan.

2 Reduce the heat slightly and add the onion, garlic, and bacon to the pan. Cook, stirring frequently, for a further 2 minutes or until the onion has softened.

3 Add the wine and simmer for 1 minute. Add the bouillon and return the rabbit to the pan with any juices. Bring to a boil and skim off any foam that rises to the surface.

4 Reduce the heat and stir in the tomato juice, tomato paste, carrots, bay leaf, thyme, and oregano. Season with salt and pepper. Cover and simmer gently for 1 hour or until very tender.

5 Remove the rabbit pieces with a draining spoon and, when cool enough to handle, remove the meat from the bones. Discard any fat or gristle, along with the bones. Cut the meat into bite-size pieces and return to the soup.

6 Melt the butter in a skillet over medium-high heat. Add the mushrooms and season with salt and pepper. Cook gently until lightly golden, then add to the soup. Simmer for 10-15 minutes to blend. Season to taste and serve sprinkled with parsley.

This delicately curried chicken soup requires a flavorful bouillon. Its velvety texture makes it an elegant starter.

Senegalese Soup

1 Heat the bouillon in a large pan. Add the onion, carrot, celery, apple, garlic, and curry powder with a large pinch of salt, if the bouillon is unsalted. Bring to a boil, reduce the heat, and simmer, covered, for 20 minutes.

2 Trim any fat from the chicken. Add the chicken to the bouillon and continue simmering for 10 minutes or until the chicken is tender. Remove the chicken with a slotted spoon.

3 Strain the bouillon and discard the bouillon vegetables. Spoon off any fat. When cool enough to handle, cut the chicken into thin slivers.

4 Put the strained bouillon in a large heavy-based pan and put over a medium heat. When starting to bubble around the edge, adjust the heat so it continues to bubble gently at the edge but remains still in the center.

5 Put the egg yolks in a bowl. Add the cornstarch and cream and whisk until smooth. Whisk one-quarter of the hot bouillon into the cream mixture, then pour it all back into the pan, whisking constantly. With a wooden spoon, stir constantly for 10 minutes or until the soup thickens slightly. Do not allow it to boil or the soup may curdle. If you see the soup beginning to boil, take the pan off the heat and stir more quickly until it cools down.

6 Stir in the chicken and reduce the heat to low. Season the soup with salt, pepper, and nutmeg. Ladle into warmed soup bowls, garnish with toasted coconut strips or pecans, and serve.

SERVES 4

5 cups chicken bouillon
1 small onion, sliced thinly
1 small carrot, chopped finely
1 celery stalk, chopped finely
½ small eating apple, peeled, cored, and chopped
1–2 garlic cloves, halved
1 tsp mild curry powder
7 oz/200 g skinless, boneless chicken breast
2 egg yolks
4 tbsp cornstarch
1 cup whipping cream
freshly grated nutmeg
salt and white pepper
toasted coconut strips or pecans, to garnish

NUTRITION
Calories 428; Sugars 6 g; Protein 16 g;
Carbohydrate 34 g; Fat 26 g; Saturates 15 g

 moderate

15 mins

 40 mins

This soup contains okra, an essential ingredient in a gumbo. It helps thicken the soup, which starts with the traditional Cajun base of cooked flour and oil.

Chicken Gumbo Soup

SERVES 6

2 tbsp olive oil
4 tbsp all-purpose flour
1 onion, chopped finely
1 small green bell pepper, cored, seeded, and finely chopped
1 celery stalk, chopped finely
5 cups chicken bouillon
14 oz/400 g canned chopped tomatoes in juice
3 garlic cloves, chopped finely or crushed
4½ oz/125 g okra, stems removed, cut into ¼-inch/5-mm thick slices
4 tbsp white rice
7 oz/200 g cooked chicken, cubed
4 oz/115 g cooked garlic sausage, sliced or cubed

1 Heat the oil in a large heavy-based pan over a medium-low heat and stir in the flour. Cook for about 15 minutes, stirring occasionally, until the mixture is a rich golden brown (see Cook's Tip).

2 Add the onion, green bell pepper, and celery and continue cooking for about 10 minutes or until the onion softens.

3 Slowly pour in the bouillon and bring to a boil, stirring well and scraping the bottom of the pan to mix in the flour. Remove the pan from the heat.

4 Add the tomatoes and garlic. Stir in the okra and rice and season. Reduce the heat, cover, and simmer for 20 minutes or until the okra is tender.

5 Add the chicken and sausage and continue simmering for about 10 minutes. Taste and adjust the seasoning, if necessary, and ladle into warmed bowls.

NUTRITION
Calories 242; Sugars 5 g; Protein 17 g;
Carbohydrate 23 g; Fat 10 g; Saturates 2 g

 easy

10 mins

1 hr

 **COOK'S TIP**

Keep a watchful eye on the roux (flour and oil) as it begins to darken. The soup gains a lot of flavor from this traditional Cajun base, but if it burns the soup will be bitter. If you prefer, omit it and start by cooking the onion, green bell pepper, and celery in the oil, adding the flour when they are softened.

América

This soup uses the colorful dried bean mixes available that include a variety of different beans. Brightly colored vegetables are added to create a lively combination.

Confetti Bean Soup

1 Pick over the beans, cover generously with cold water, and leave to soak for 6 hours or overnight. Drain the beans, put in a pan, and add enough cold water to cover by 2 inches/5 cm. Bring to a boil and boil for 10 minutes, skimming off the foam as it accumulates. Drain and rinse well.

2 Heat the oil in a large pan over a medium heat. Add the onions and bell pepper, cover, and cook for 3–4 minutes, stirring occasionally, until the onion is just softened. Add the garlic, carrots, parsnip, celery, and gammon or ham and continue cooking for 2–3 minutes or until the onion begins to color.

3 Add the water, drained beans, tomato paste, thyme, and bay leaf. Bring just to a boil, cover, and simmer, occasionally stirring, for 1¼ hours or until the beans and vegetables are tender.

4 Put the potato in a small pan and ladle over just enough of the bean cooking liquid to cover the potatoes. Bring to a boil, cover the pan, reduce the heat, and boil gently for about 12 minutes or until the potato is very tender.

5 Put the potato and its cooking liquid into a blender or food processor, then add 3 ladlefuls of the beans with a small amount of their liquid and purée until completely smooth.

6 Scrape the purée into the pan, add the marjoram and parsley, and stir to blend. Season the soup to taste. Reheat gently over a medium–low heat and ladle the soup into warmed bowls.

SERVES 8

1 lb 2 oz/500 g mixed dried beans
1 tbsp olive oil
2 onions, chopped finely
1 yellow or orange bell pepper, cored, seeded, and finely chopped
3 garlic cloves, chopped finely or crushed
2 carrots, cubed
1 parsnip, cubed
2 celery stalks, halved lengthways and cut into ¼-inch/5-mm pieces
3½ oz/100 g lean smoked gammon or ham, cubed
8 cups water
2 tbsp tomato paste
⅛ tsp dried thyme
1 bay leaf
1 potato, diced finely
1 tbsp chopped fresh marjoram
2 tbsp chopped fresh parsley
salt and pepper

NUTRITION
Calories 241; Sugars 6 g; Protein 16 g; Carbohydrate 41 g; Fat 2 g; Saturates 0 g

 moderate
 6 hrs 15 mins
1 hr 45 mins

Pumpkin, a greatly underrated vegetable, balances the spicy heat in this soup and gives it a splash of color, too.

Bean *and* Pumpkin Soup

SERVES 4

1½ cups dried kidney beans
1 tbsp olive oil
2 onions, chopped finely
4 garlic cloves, chopped finely
1 celery stalk, sliced thinly
1 carrot, halved and thinly sliced
2 tsp tomato paste
pinch of dried thyme
pinch of dried oregano
pinch of ground cumin
5 cups water
1 bay leaf
14 oz/400 g canned chopped tomatoes
2 cups peeled diced pumpkin flesh
¼ tsp chili paste
salt and pepper
fresh cilantro leaves, to garnish

1 Pick over the beans, cover generously with cold water, and set aside to soak for 6 hours or overnight. Drain the beans, put in a pan, and add enough cold water to cover by 2 inches/5 cm. Bring to a boil and boil for 10 minutes. Drain and rinse.

2 Heat the olive oil in a large pan over medium heat. Add the onions and cook, stirring occasionally, for 3–4 minutes or until they are just softened. Add the garlic, celery, and carrot and continue cooking for 2 minutes.

3 Add the kidney beans, tomato paste, thyme, oregano, cumin, water, and bay leaf. When the mixture is just beginning to simmer, reduce the heat to low. Cover and simmer gently, stirring occasionally, for 1 hour.

4 Stir in the chopped tomatoes, pumpkin, and chili paste. Continue simmering, stirring occasionally, for approximately 1 hour or until the beans and pumpkin are tender.

5 Season the soup to taste with salt and pepper and stir in a little more chili paste if liked. Ladle the soup into warmed bowls, garnish with cilantro leaves, and serve immediately.

NUTRITION
Calories *170*; Sugars *8 g*; Protein *11 g*;
Carbohydrate *27 g*; Fat *3 g*; Saturates *0 g*

easy

6 hrs 15 mins

2 hrs 30 mins

This soup is satisfying and very healthy. Brown rice gives a pleasing chewy texture, but white rice could be used instead.

Rice *and* Black-Eye Pea Soup

1 Put the peas in a bowl, cover generously with cold water, and set aside to soak for at least 6 hours or overnight. Drain the peas, put in a pan, and add enough cold water to cover by 2 inches/5 cm. Bring to a boil and boil for 10 minutes. Drain and rinse well.

2 Heat the oil in a large heavy pan over medium heat. Add the onion, cover, and cook, stirring frequently, for 3–4 minutes or until just softened. Add the garlic, carrots, celery, and bell pepper, stir well, and cook for a further 2 minutes.

3 Transfer to a larger pan if necessary. Add the peas, ham, thyme, bay leaf, bouillon, and water. Bring to a boil, reduce the heat, cover, and simmer gently, stirring occasionally, for 1 hour or until the peas are just tender.

4 Stir in the rice and season the soup with salt, if needed, and pepper. Continue cooking for 30 minutes or until the rice and peas are tender.

5 Remove and discard the bay leaf. Taste the soup and adjust the seasoning if necessary. Ladle into warmed bowls and serve garnished with parsley or chives.

SERVES 4

2¾ cups dried black-eye peas
1 tbsp olive oil
1 large onion, chopped finely
2 garlic cloves, chopped finely or crushed
2 carrots, chopped finely
2 celery stalks, chopped finely
1 small red bell pepper, seeded and finely chopped
½ cup finely diced lean smoked ham
½ tsp fresh thyme leaves
1 bay leaf
5 cups chicken or vegetable bouillon
2½ cups water
½ cup brown rice
salt and pepper
chopped fresh parsley or chives, to garnish

NUTRITION
Calories *285*; Sugars *7 g*; Protein *18 g*; Carbohydrate *43 g*; Fat *5 g*; Saturates *1 g*

easy

6 hrs 15 mins

2 hrs

Traditional Soups

The range of soups found in this chapter will provide good old-fashioned nourishment and are perfect served as a main course accompanied by a hearty chunk of fresh bread or perhaps a salad or a wedge of strong tasting cheese. Wholesome treats include the traditional Scots recipe for Partan Bree, lentil and ham soup, and delicious mushroom soup. To make the most of these soups, remember that they are only as good as their ingredients, so be sure to pick good quality produce.

SOUPS

It is difficult to imagine that celery root, a coarse, knobbly vegetable, can taste so sweet. It makes a delicious soup.

Celery Root *and* Potato Soup

SERVES 4

1 tbsp butter
1 onion, chopped
2 large leeks, halved lengthwise and sliced
1 lb 10 oz/750 g celery root, peeled and cubed
8 oz/225 g potatoes, cubed
1 carrot, quartered and thinly sliced
5 cups water
pinch of dried marjoram
1 bay leaf
freshly grated nutmeg
salt and pepper
celery leaves, to garnish

1 Melt the butter in a large pan over medium–low heat. Add the onion and leeks and cook, stirring frequently, until just softened; do not let color.

2 Add the celery root, potatoes, carrot, water, marjoram, and bay leaf with a pinch of salt. Bring to a boil, reduce the heat, cover, and simmer for about 25 minutes or until the vegetables are tender. Remove and discard the bay leaf.

3 Let the soup cool slightly. Transfer to a blender or food processor and process until smooth. (If using a food processor, strain off the cooking liquid and reserve. Purée the soup solids with enough cooking liquid to moisten them, then combine with the remaining liquid.)

4 Return the puréed soup to the pan. Stir to blend the ingredients thoroughly. Season the soup with nutmeg, salt, and pepper to taste, then simmer over medium–low heat until it is reheated.

5 Ladle the soup into warmed bowls, garnish with celery leaves, and then serve immediately.

NUTRITION
Calories *127*; Sugars *8 g*; Protein *4 g*;
Carbohydrate *17 g*; Fat *4 g*; Saturates *2 g*

 moderate

 10 mins

35 mins

This unusual baked soup is perfect for lunch on a crisp, cold winter day—pop it in the oven and enjoy a brisk walk while it is cooking.

Baked Leek *and* Cabbage Soup

1 Melt the butter in a large pan over medium heat. Add the leeks and onion and cook for 4–5 minutes, stirring frequently, until just soft.

2 Add the garlic and cabbage, stir to combine, and continue cooking for about 5 minutes to wilt the cabbage.

3 Stir in the bouillon and simmer for 10 minutes. Taste and season with salt and pepper.

4 Arrange the bread in the base of a large, deep, 12-cup ovenproof dish. Sprinkle about half the grated cheese over the bread.

5 Ladle over the soup and top with the remaining grated cheese. Bake in a preheated oven at 350°F/180°C for 1 hour. Serve at once.

SERVES 4

2 tbsp butter

2 large leeks, halved lengthwise and thinly sliced

1 large onion, halved and sliced thinly

3 garlic cloves, chopped finely

2 cups finely shredded green cabbage

4 cups vegetable bouillon

4 slices firm bread, cut in half, or 8 slices baguette

2 cups grated Swiss cheese

NUTRITION

Calories *420*; Sugars *8 g*; Protein *24 g*; Carbohydrate *27 g*; Fat *25 g*; Saturates *15 g*

   moderate

15 mins

1 hr 25 mins

👨‍🍳 **COOK'S TIP**

A large soufflé dish or earthenware casserole at least 4 inches/10 cm deep, or an enamelled cast-iron casserole, is good for baking the soup. If the soup fills the dish to the top, put a cookie sheet with a rim underneath to catch any overflow.

A quick, chunky soup, ideal for a snack or a quick lunch. Save some of the soup and purée it to make one portion of creamed soup for the next day.

Leek, Potato, *and* Carrot Soup

SERVES 2

1 leek, about 6 oz/175 g
1 tbsp sunflower oil
1 garlic clove, crushed
3 cups vegetable bouillon
1 bay leaf
1/4 tsp ground cumin
1 1/2 cups diced potatoes
generous 1/2 cup coarsely grated carrot
salt and pepper
chopped parsley, to garnish

pureed soup
5–6 tbsp milk
1–2 tbsp heavy or sour cream

NUTRITION
Calories *156*; Sugars *7 g*; Protein *4 g*;
Carbohydrate *22 g*; Fat *6 g*; Saturates *0.7 g*

 very easy

 10 mins

 25 mins

1 Trim off and discard some of the coarse green part of the leek, then slice thinly, and rinse thoroughly in cold water. Drain well.

2 Heat the sunflower oil in a heavy pan. Add the leek and garlic and cook over low heat for about 2–3 minutes or until soft, but barely colored. Add the bouillon, bay leaf, and cumin and season to taste with salt and pepper. Bring to a boil, stirring constantly.

3 Add the diced potato to the pan, cover, and simmer over low heat for 10–15 minutes. Keep a careful eye on the soup during the cooking time to make sure the potato cooks until it is just tender, but not broken up.

4 Add the grated carrot to the pan and simmer the soup for a further 2–3 minutes. Adjust the seasoning if necessary, discard the bay leaf, and serve the soup in warmed bowls, sprinkled liberally with the chopped parsley.

5 To make a puréed soup, first process the leftovers (about half the original soup) in a blender or food processor until smooth, or press through a strainer with the back of a wooden spoon, and then return to a clean pan. Add the milk to the soup, bring to a boil, and simmer for 2–3 minutes.

6 Adjust the seasoning and stir in the heavy cream or sour cream, before serving the soup in warmed bowls, sprinkled with chopped parsley.

Cauliflower can taste rather bland, but using hard cider in this soup gives it an unusual kick.

Cauliflower *and* Cider Soup

1 Melt the butter in a pan over medium heat. Add the onion and garlic and cook for about 5 minutes, stirring occasionally, until just soft.

2 Add the carrot and cauliflower to the pan and pour over the cider. Season with salt, pepper, and a generous grating of nutmeg. Bring to a boil, then reduce the heat to low. Cover and cook gently for about 50 minutes or until the vegetables are very soft.

3 Let the soup cool slightly, then transfer to a blender or food processor and purée until smooth, working in batches if necessary. (If using a food processor, strain off the cooking liquid and reserve. Purée the soup solids with enough cooking liquid to moisten them, then combine with the remaining liquid.)

4 Return the soup to the pan and stir in the milk and cream. Taste and adjust the seasoning, if necessary. Simmer the soup over low heat, stirring occasionally, until heated through.

5 Ladle the soup into warmed bowls, garnish with chives, and serve.

SERVES 4

2 tbsp butter
1 onion, chopped finely
1 garlic clove, crushed
1 carrot, sliced thinly
5 cups cauliflower flowerets
2½ cups hard cider
freshly grated nutmeg
½ cup milk
½ cup heavy cream
salt and pepper
snipped chives, to garnish

NUTRITION
Calories 312; Sugars 13 g; Protein 7 g; Carbohydrate 15 g; Fat 21 g; Saturates 13 g

 moderate
15 mins
 1 hr

COOK'S TIP

If you don't have hard cider, substitute generous ¾ cup each white wine, apple juice, and water.

Fresh asparagus is now available for most of the year, so this soup can be made at any time, although it can also be made using canned asparagus.

Asparagus Soup

SERVES 4

1 bunch asparagus, about 12 oz/350 g, or
   2 packs mini asparagus, about 5½ oz/
   150 g each
3 cups vegetable bouillon
¼ cup butter or margarine
1 onion, chopped
3 tbsp all-purpose flour
¼ tsp ground coriander
1 tbsp lemon juice
2 cups milk
4–6 tbsp heavy or light cream
salt and pepper

1 Wash and trim the asparagus, discarding the lower, woody part of the stem. Cut the remainder into short lengths, keeping aside a few tips to use as a garnish. Mini asparagus does not need to be trimmed.

2 Cook the tips in the minimum of boiling salted water for 5–10 minutes. Drain and set aside.

3 Put the asparagus in a pan with the bouillon, bring to a boil, cover, and simmer for about 20 minutes or until soft. Drain and reserve the bouillon.

4 Melt the butter or margarine in a pan. Add the onion and cook over low heat until soft, but only barely colored. Stir in the flour and cook for 1 minute, then gradually whisk in the reserved bouillon, and bring to a boil.

5 Simmer for 2–3 minutes or until thickened, then stir in the cooked asparagus, seasoning, coriander, and lemon juice. Simmer for 10 minutes, then cool a little, and either press through a strainer with the back of a spoon or process in a blender or food processor until smooth.

6 Pour into a clean pan, add the milk and reserved asparagus tips, and bring to a boil. Simmer for 2 minutes. Stir in the cream, reheat gently, and serve.

NUTRITION

Calories *196*; Sugars *7 g*; Protein *7 g*; Carbohydrate *15 g*; Fat *12 g*; Saturates *4 g*

 very easy

5–10 mins

55 mins

COOK'S TIP

If using canned asparagus, drain off the liquid and use as part of the measured bouillon. Remove a few small asparagus tips for garnish and chop the remainder. Continue as above.

This old-fashioned soup is nourishing and warming, with distinctive flavors and a nice chewy texture.

Mushroom *and* Barley Soup

1 Rinse and drain the barley. Bring 2 cups of the bouillon to a boil in a small pan. Add the bay leaf and a pinch of salt. Stir in the barley, reduce the heat, cover, and simmer for 40 minutes.

2 Melt the butter in a large skillet over a medium heat. Add the mushrooms and season to taste with salt and pepper. Cook, stirring occasionally, for about 8 minutes or until they are golden brown. Stir more often after the mushrooms start to color. Remove the skillet from the heat.

3 Heat the oil in a large pan over medium heat and add the onion and carrots. Cook, stirring occasionally, for about 3 minutes or until the onion is softened and translucent.

4 Add the remaining bouillon and bring to a boil. Stir in the barley with its cooking liquid and add the mushrooms. Reduce the heat, cover, and simmer gently, stirring occasionally, for about 20 minutes.

5 Stir in the tarragon and parsley. Ladle into warmed bowls, garnish with fresh parsley or tarragon, and serve.

SERVES 4

¼ cup pearl barley
6¾ cups chicken or vegetable bouillon
1 bay leaf
1 tbsp butter
12 oz/350 g mushrooms, sliced thinly
1 tsp olive oil
1 onion, chopped finely
2 carrots, sliced thinly
1 tbsp chopped fresh tarragon
1 tbsp chopped fresh parsley
salt and pepper
few fresh parsley or tarragon sprigs, to garnish

COOK'S TIP

The barley will continue to absorb liquid if the soup is stored, so if you are making ahead, you may need to add a little more bouillon or water when reheating the soup.

NUTRITION
Calories *204*; Sugars *7 g*; Protein *5 g*; Carbohydrate *31 g*; Fat *8 g*; Saturates *3 g*

      moderate

5 mins

1 hr 15 mins

Crisp, fresh celery and creamy Stilton cheese are a delicious combination, which works equally well in soup.

Celery *and* Stilton Soup

SERVES 4

2 tbsp butter
1 onion, chopped finely
4 large celery stalks, peeled and finely chopped
1 large carrot, chopped finely
4 cups vegetable bouillon
3–4 thyme sprigs
1 bay leaf
½ cup heavy cream
1¼ cups crumbled Stilton cheese
freshly grated nutmeg
salt and pepper
celery leaves, to garnish

1 Melt the butter in a large pan over a medium-low heat. Add the onion and cook for 3–4 minutes, stirring frequently, until just soft. Add the celery and carrot and continue cooking for 3 minutes. Season lightly with salt and pepper.

2 Add the bouillon, thyme, and bay leaf and bring to a boil. Reduce the heat, cover, and simmer gently for about 25 minutes, stirring occasionally, until the vegetables are very tender.

3 Let the soup cool slightly and remove the thyme and bay leaf. Transfer the soup to a blender or food processor and purée until smooth, working in batches, if necessary. (If using a food processor, strain off the cooking liquid and reserve. Purée the soup solids with enough cooking liquid to moisten them, then combine with the remaining liquid.)

4 Return the puréed soup to the pan and stir in the cream. Simmer over a low heat for 5 minutes.

5 Add the Stilton slowly, stirring constantly, until smooth. (Do not let the soup boil.) Taste and adjust the seasoning, adding salt, if needed, plenty of pepper, and nutmeg to taste.

6 Ladle into warmed bowls, garnish with celery leaves, and serve.

NUTRITION

Calories *381*; Sugars *6 g*; Protein *10 g*; Carbohydrate *7 g*; Fat *35 g*; Saturates *21 g*

 moderate

15 mins

40 mins

The cooking liquid in which the fish is poached becomes a delicious fish bouillon. If you just want bouillon, poach fish heads and trimmings instead of a whole fish.

Trout *and* Celery Root Soup

1 To make the fish bouillon base, melt the butter in a fish kettle, a large pan, or cast-iron casserole over a medium-high heat. Add the onion, carrot, and leek and cook for about 3 minutes or until the onion starts to soften.

2 Add the wine, water, and bay leaf. Bring to a boil, reduce the heat a little, cover, and boil gently for 15 minutes.

3 Put the fish into the liquid (if necessary, cut the fish in pieces to fit in). Bring back to a boil and skim off any foam that rises to the top. Reduce the heat to low and simmer gently for 20 minutes.

4 Remove the fish and set aside. Strain the bouillon through a cheesecloth-lined strainer into a clean pan. Remove any fat from the bouillon. (There should be about 6 cups bouillon.)

5 Bring the bouillon to a boil. Add the celery root and boil gently, uncovered, for 15–20 minutes or until it is tender and the liquid has reduced by about one-third.

6 When the fish is cool enough to handle, peel off the skin and remove the flesh from the bones. Discard the skin, bones, head, and tail.

7 Add the cream to the soup and when it comes back to a boil, stir in the dissolved cornstarch. Boil gently for 2–3 minutes or until slightly thickened, stirring frequently. Return the fish to the soup. Cook for 3–4 minutes to reheat. Taste and adjust the seasoning, if necessary. Ladle into warmed bowls and garnish with chervil or parsley.

SERVES 4

1 lb 9 oz/700 g whole trout
7 oz/200 g celery root, peeled and diced
¼ cup heavy cream
3 tbsp cornstarch, dissolved in 3 tbsp water
chopped fresh chervil or parsley, to garnish

fish bouillon base
1 tbsp butter
l onion, sliced thinly
l carrot, sliced thinly
l leek, sliced thinly
l cup dry white wine
5 cups water
1 bay leaf

NUTRITION
Calories *369*; Sugars *4 g*; Protein *0 24*; Carbohydrate *17 g*; Fat *21 g*; Saturates *10 g*

 moderate

 25 mins

1 hr 15 mins

Salmon is a favorite with almost everyone. This delicately flavored and pretty soup is perfect for entertaining.

Salmon *and* Leek Soup

SERVES 4

1 tbsp olive oil

1 large onion, finely chopped

3 large leeks, including green parts, thinly sliced

1 potato, finely diced

2 cups fish bouillon

3 cups water

1 bay leaf

10½ oz/300 g skinless salmon fillet, cut into ½-inch/1-cm cubes

5 tbsp heavy cream

salt and pepper

fresh lemon juice, optional

snipped fresh chervil or parsley, to garnish

1 Heat the oil in a heavy-based pan over a medium heat. Add the onion and leeks and cook for about 3 minutes or until they begin to soften.

2 Add the potato, bouillon, water, and bay leaf with a large pinch of salt. Bring to a boil, reduce the heat, cover, and cook gently for about 25 minutes or until the vegetables are tender. Remove the bay leaf.

3 Allow the soup to cool slightly, then transfer about half of it to a blender or food processor and purée until smooth. (If using a food processor, strain off the cooking liquid and reserve. Purée half the soup solids with enough cooking liquid to moisten them, then combine with the remaining liquid.)

4 Return the puréed soup to the pan and stir to blend. Reheat gently over a medium-low heat.

5 Season the salmon with salt and pepper and add to the soup. Continue cooking for about 5 minutes, stirring occasionally, until the fish is tender and starts to break up. Stir in the cream, taste and adjust the seasoning, adding a little lemon juice if wished. Ladle into warmed bowls, sprinkle with chervil or parsley and serve.

NUTRITION

Calories *338*; Sugars *7 g*; Protein *19 g*; Carbohydrate *17 g*; Fat *22 g*; Saturates *8 g*

 moderate

 10–15 mins

40 mins

This delicious soup utilizes every part of the shrimp. If you wish, you could even leave the shrimp flesh out of the soup because most of the flavor comes from the shells.

Shrimp Bisque

1 Peel the shrimp and keep the shells for the soup. Reserve the shrimp flesh, covered, in the refrigerator.

2 Heat the oil in a large pan. Add the shrimp shells and cook over a high heat, stirring frequently, until they start to brown. Reduce the heat and add one-quarter of the onions, the carrot, celery, and garlic. Cover and cook for 4–5 minutes, stirring frequently, until the onions soften. Add the water and bay leaf with a small pinch of salt. Bring to a boil, reduce the heat, cover, and simmer gently for 25 minutes. Strain the shrimp bouillon.

3 Heat the butter in a large pan over a medium heat and add the remaining onions. Cover and cook for 5–6 minutes, stirring frequently, until they soften and just begin to color. Add the shrimp bouillon, rice, and tomato paste. Bring to a boil. Reduce the heat, cover, and simmer for 30 minutes or until rice is very soft.

4 Allow the soup to cool slightly, then transfer to a blender or food processor and purée until smooth, working in batches if necessary. (If using a food processor, strain off the cooking liquid and reserve. Purée the soup solids with enough cooking liquid to moisten them, then combine with the remaining liquid.)

5 Return the soup to the pan and place over a medium-low heat. Add the reserved shrimp and a few drops of lemon juice. Simmer for about 8 minutes, stirring occasionally, until the soup is reheated. Taste and adjust the seasoning. Ladle into warmed bowls, sprinkle with dill or parsley and serve.

SERVES 4

1 lb 2 oz/500 g cooked shrimp in the shell
2 tsp oil
2 large onions, halved and sliced
1 carrot, grated
1 celery stalk, sliced
1–2 garlic cloves, chopped finely or crushed
6 cups water
1 bay leaf
2 tsp butter
6 tbsp white rice
1 tbsp tomato paste
fresh lemon juice
salt and pepper
snipped fresh dill or chopped parsley, to garnish

NUTRITION
Calories 227; Sugars 7 g; Protein 25 g; Carbohydrate 22 g; Fat 4 g; Saturates 1 g

✪✪✪   moderate
     15 mins
     1 hr 20 mins

This light, lean soup is studded with fragrant herbs and small diced vegetables. The bouillon may be used as a basis for other soups.

Beef Broth

SERVES 4

7 oz/200 g celery root, diced finely
2 large carrots, diced finely
2 tsp chopped fresh marjoram
2 tsp chopped fresh parsley
2 plum tomatoes, peeled, seeded, and diced
salt and pepper

beef bouillon

1 lb 4 oz/550 g boneless beef shin or stewing
   steak, cut into large cubes
1 lb 10 oz/750 g veal, beef, or pork bones
2 onions, quartered
2½ quarts water
4 garlic cloves, sliced
2 carrots, sliced
1 large leek, sliced
1 celery stalk, cut into 2-inch/5-cm pieces
1 bay leaf
4–5 fresh thyme sprigs or ¼ tsp dried thyme
salt

NUTRITION

Calories *21*; Sugars *3 g*; Protein *1 g*;
Carbohydrate *4 g*; Fat *1 g*; Saturates *0 g*

⊛⊛⊛   moderate

    15 mins

    5 hrs 15 mins

1 To make the bouillon, trim the fat from the beef and put the beef and the fat into a large roasting pan with the bones and onions. Roast in a preheated oven, 375°F/190°C, for 30–40 minutes or until browned, turning once or twice. Transfer the ingredients to a large flameproof casserole and then discard the beef fat.

2 Add the water (it should cover by at least 2 inches/5 cm) and bring to a boil. Skim off any foam, reduce the heat, and add the garlic, carrots, leek, celery, bay leaf, thyme, and a pinch of salt. Simmer very gently for 4 hours, skimming occasionally. If the ingredients emerge from the liquid, top up with water.

3 Strain the bouillon through a cheesecloth-lined strainer into a large container and remove as much fat as possible. Discard the bones and vegetables, but save the meat if wished.

4 Boil the bouillon very gently until it is reduced to 6½ cups. Taste and adjust the seasoning if necessary.

5 Bring a pan of salted water to a boil and add the celery root and carrots. Reduce the heat, cover, and simmer for 15 minutes or until tender. Drain.

6 Add the herbs to the boiling beef bouillon. Divide the cooked vegetables and tomatoes among warmed bowls, ladle over the bouillon, and serve.

This traditional winter soup is full of goodness, with lots of tasty golden vegetables along with tender barley and lamb.

Scotch Broth

1 Rinse the barley under cold running water. Put in a pan and add water to cover generously. Bring to a boil over medium heat and boil for 3 minutes, skimming off the foam from the surface. Remove the pan from the heat, cover, and set aside.

2 Put the lamb in another large pan with the measured water and bring to a boil. Skim off the foam that rises to the surface.

3 Stir in the garlic, bouillon, onion, and bay leaf. Reduce the heat, partially cover, and simmer for 15 minutes.

4 Drain the barley and add to the soup. Add the leek, carrots, parsnip, and rutabaga. Simmer, stirring occasionally, for about 1 hour or until the lamb and vegetables are tender.

5 Season to taste with salt and pepper, stir in the parsley, and serve.

SERVES 4

¼ cup pearl barley
10½ oz/300 g lean boneless lamb, such as shoulder fillet, trimmed of fat and cut into ½-inch/1-cm cubes
3 cups water
2 garlic cloves, chopped finely or crushed
4 cups chicken or meat bouillon
1 onion, chopped finely
1 bay leaf
1 large leek, quartered lengthwise and sliced
2 large carrots, finely diced
1 parsnip, finely diced
4½ oz/125 g rutabaga, diced
2 tbsp chopped fresh parsley
salt and pepper

NUTRITION

Calories *186*; Sugars *6 g*; Protein *13 g*; Carbohydrate *23 g*; Fat *5 g*; Saturates *2 g*

 moderate

 10–15 mins

1 hr 30 mins

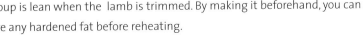

COOK'S TIP

This soup is lean when the lamb is trimmed. By making it beforehand, you can remove any hardened fat before reheating.

A thick vegetable soup which is a delicious meal in itself. Serve the soup with thin shavings of Parmesan and warm ciabatta bread.

Winter Soup

SERVES 4

2 tbsp olive oil
2 leeks, sliced thinly
2 zucchini, chopped
2 garlic cloves, crushed
4 cups canned chopped tomatoes
1 tbsp tomato paste
1 bay leaf
3½ cups vegetable bouillon
3½ cups canned garbanzo beans, drained
8 oz/225 g spinach
1 oz/25 g Parmesan cheese, shaved thinly
salt and pepper
crusty bread, to serve

1 Heat the oil in a heavy pan. Add the sliced leeks and zucchini and cook over a medium heat, stirring constantly, for 5 minutes.

2 Add the garlic, chopped tomatoes, tomato paste, bay leaf, vegetable bouillon, and garbanzo beans. Bring to a boil, reduce the heat, and simmer, stirring occasionally, for 5 minutes.

3 Shred the spinach finely and add it to the soup. Cook the soup for a further 2 minutes over medium-high heat, until the spinach is just wilted. Season to taste with salt and pepper.

4 Remove the bay leaf. Pour the soup into a warmed tureen or individual bowls and sprinkle over the Parmesan. Serve with crusty bread.

NUTRITION
Calories *285*; Sugars *11 g*; Protein *16 g*;
Carbohydrate *29 g*; Fat *12 g*; Saturates *3 g*

very easy

10 mins

20 mins

Warming and nutritious, this broth is perfect for a cold winter's day. The slow cooking allows you to use one of the cheaper cuts of meat.

Lamb *and* Barley Broth

1 Heat the vegetable oil in a large, heavy-based pan and add the pieces of lamb, turning them to seal and brown on both sides.

2 Lift the lamb out of the pan and set aside until required.

3 Add the onion, carrots, and leeks to the pan and cook gently for about 3 minutes.

4 Return the lamb to the pan and add the vegetable bouillon, bay leaf, parsley, and pearl barley to the pan.

5 Bring the mixture in the pan to a boil, then reduce the heat. Cover and simmer for 1½ –2 hours.

6 Discard the parsley sprigs. Lift the pieces of lamb from the broth and allow them to cool slightly.

7 Remove the bones and any fat and chop the meat. Return the lamb to the broth and reheat gently.

8 Ladle the lamb and barley broth into warmed bowls and serve immediately.

SERVES 4

1 tbsp vegetable oil
1 lb 2 oz/500 g lean neck of lamb
1 large onion, sliced
2 carrots, sliced
2 leeks, sliced
4 cups vegetable bouillon
1 bay leaf
few sprigs of fresh parsley
⅓ cup pearl barley

NUTRITION
Calories *304*; Sugars *4 g*; Protein *29 g*; Carbohydrate *16 g*; Fat *14 g*; Saturates *6 g*

easy

15 mins

2 hrs 15 mins

👨‍🍳 COOK'S TIP

This broth will taste even better if made the day before, as this allows the flavors to fully develop. It also means that any fat will solidify on the surface so you can then lift it off. Keep the broth in the refrigerator until required.

Smooth and delicious, this soup has the most glorious golden color and a fabulous flavor.

Lentil *and* Parsnip Pottage

SERVES 4

3 slices lean bacon, chopped
1 onion, chopped
2 carrots, chopped
2 parsnips, chopped
⅓ cup red lentils
4 cups vegetable bouillon or water
salt and pepper
chopped fresh chives to garnish

1 Heat a large pan, add the bacon, and dry-fry for 5 minutes or until the bacon is crisp and golden.

2 Add the chopped onion, carrots, and parsnips and cook for about 5 minutes without browning.

3 Add the lentils to the pan and stir to mix with the vegetables.

4 Add the bouillon or water to the pan and bring to a boil. Cover and simmer for 30–40 minutes or until tender.

5 Transfer the soup to a blender or food processor and blend for about 15 seconds or until smooth. Alternatively, press the soup through a strainer.

6 Return to the pan and reheat gently until almost boiling.

7 Season the soup with salt and pepper to taste.

8 Garnish the lentil and parsnip pottage with chopped fresh chives and serve at once.

NUTRITION
Calories *82*; Sugars *4 g*; Protein *6 g*; Carbohydrate *13 g*; Fat *1 g*; Saturates *0.3 g*

 very easy

5 mins

 55 mins

COOK'S TIP

For a meatier soup, use a ham hock in place of the bacon. Cook it for 1½–2 hours before adding the vegetables and lentils and use the ham's cooking liquid as the bouillon.

This is a good hearty soup, based on a bouillon made from a ham hock, with plenty of vegetables and red lentils to thicken it and add flavor.

Lentil *and* Ham Soup

1 Put the lentils and bouillon or water in a pan and set aside to soak for 1–2 hours.

2 Add the onions, garlic, carrots, ham hock or chopped bacon, tomatoes, and bay leaves. Season to taste with salt and pepper.

3 Bring the mixture to a boil over medium heat, then lower the heat, cover, and simmer for about 1 hour or until the lentils are tender, stirring occasionally to prevent the lentils from sticking to the bottom of the pan.

4 Add the potatoes and continue to simmer for about 20 minutes or until the potatoes and the meat on the ham hock are tender.

5 Remove and discard the bay leaves. Remove the ham hock and chop 1 cup of the meat and reserve. If liked, press half the soup through a strainer or process in a food processor or blender until smooth. Return to the pan with the rest of the soup.

6 Adjust the seasoning, add the vinegar and allspice, and the reserved chopped ham. Simmer gently for a further 5–10 minutes. Serve sprinkled liberally with scallions or chopped parsley.

SERVES 4

1 cup red lentils
6¼ cups bouillon or water
2 onions, chopped
1 garlic clove, crushed
2 large carrots, chopped
1 lean ham hock or 6 oz/175 g lean bacon, chopped
4 large tomatoes, peeled and chopped
2 bay leaves
9 oz/250 g potatoes, chopped
1 tbsp white wine vinegar
¼ tsp ground allspice
salt and pepper
chopped scallions or fresh parsley, to garnish

NUTRITION
Calories 219; Sugars 4 g; Protein 17 g; Carbohydrate 33 g; Fat 3 g; Saturates 1 g

easy

2 hrs 15 mins

1 hr 45 mins

This is a real winter warmer—pieces of tender beef and chunky mixed vegetables are cooked in a bouillon flavored with dry sherry.

Chunky Potato *and* Beef Soup

SERVES 4

2 tbsp vegetable oil
8 oz/225 g lean braising or frying steak,
   cut into strips
8 oz/225 g new potatoes, halved
1 carrot, diced
2 celery stalks, sliced
2 leeks, sliced
3¾ cups beef bouillon
8 baby corn cobs, sliced
1 bouquet garni
2 tbsp dry sherry
salt and pepper
chopped fresh parsley, to garnish
crusty bread, to serve

1 Heat the vegetable oil in a large pan. Add the strips of steak to the pan and cook for 3 minutes, turning constantly.

2 Add the halved potatoes, diced carrot, and sliced celery and leeks. Cook, stirring constantly, for a further 5 minutes.

3 Pour in the beef bouillon and bring to a boil over medium heat. Reduce the heat until the liquid is simmering gently, then add the sliced baby corn cobs and the bouquet garni.

4 Cook the soup for a further 20 minutes or until the meat and all the vegetables are tender.

5 Remove the bouquet garni from the pan and discard. Stir the dry sherry into the soup and then season to taste with salt and pepper.

6 Pour the soup into warmed soup bowls and garnish with the chopped fresh parsley. Serve immediately with crusty bread.

NUTRITION
Calories *187*; Sugars *3 g*; Protein *14 g*;
Carbohydrate *12 g*; Fat *9 g*; Saturates *2 g*

⭐⭐   easy
🕐   5 mins
🕐   35 mins

COOK'S TIP

Make double the quantity of soup and freeze the remainder in a rigid container for later use. When ready to use, place in the refrigerator to thaw thoroughly, then heat until piping hot.

Smoked haddock gives this soup a wonderfully rich flavor, while the mashed potatoes and cream thicken and enrich the bouillon.

Smoked Haddock Soup

1 Put the fish, onion, garlic, and water into a pan. Bring to a boil, cover, and simmer over low heat for 15–20 minutes.

2 Remove the fish from the pan. Strip off the skin and remove all the bones, and reserve both. Flake the flesh finely with a fork.

3 Return the skin and bones to the pan and simmer for 10 minutes. Strain, discarding the skin and bones. Pour the cooking liquid into a clean pan.

4 Add the milk and flaked fish and season to taste with salt and pepper. Bring to a boil and simmer for about 3 minutes.

5 Gradually whisk in sufficient mashed potato to give a fairly thick soup, then stir in the butter, and sharpen to taste with lemon juice.

6 Add the yogurt and 3 tablespoons of the chopped parsley. Reheat gently and adjust the seasoning if necessary. Sprinkle with the remaining parsley and serve the soup immediately.

SERVES 4

8 oz/225 g smoked haddock fillet
1 onion, chopped finely
1 garlic clove, crushed
2½ cups water
2½ cups skim milk
3–4 cups hot mashed potatoes
2 tbsp butter
about 1 tbsp lemon juice
6 tbsp lowfat plain yogurt
4 tbsp fresh parsley, chopped
salt and pepper

NUTRITION
Calories *169*; Sugars *8 g*; Protein *16 g*; Carbohydrate *16 g*; Fat *5 g*; Saturates *3 g*

  easy

25 mins

 40 mins

COOK'S TIP

Undyed smoked haddock may be used in place of the bright yellow fish; it will give a paler color, but just as much flavor. Alternatively, use smoked cod or smoked whiting.

Lowfat Soups

Soups are traditional first course, but served with fresh crusty bread they can be a satisfying meal in their own right—and depending on the choice of ingredients—one that is low in calories. For the best results, use homemade bouillon from the liquid left over from cooking vegetables and the juices from casseroles. Potatoes can also be added to the soup to thicken it as opposed to the traditional thickeners of flour or fat and water.

Serve this soup over ice on a warm summer day as a refreshing starter. It has the fresh tang of yogurt and a dash of spice from the Tabasco sauce.

Chilled Cucumber Soup

SERVES 4

1 cucumber, peeled and diced
1²⁄₃ cups Fresh Fish Bouillon, chilled (see page 14)
²⁄₃ cup tomato juice
²⁄₃ cup lowfat plain yogurt
²⁄₃ cup lowfat fromage frais (or double the quantity of yogurt)
4¹⁄₂ oz/125 g peeled shrimp, thawed if frozen, chopped roughly
few drops Tabasco sauce
1 tbsp fresh mint, chopped
salt and white pepper
ice cubes, to serve

to garnish
sprigs of mint
cucumber slices
whole peeled shrimp

1 Place the diced cucumber in a blender or food processor and work for a few seconds until smooth. Alternatively, chop the cucumber finely and push through a strainer.

2 Transfer the cucumber to a bowl. Stir in the bouillon, tomato juice, yogurt, fromage frais (if using), and shrimp, and mix well.

3 Add the Tabasco sauce and season to taste.

4 Stir in the chopped mint, cover, and chill for at least 2 hours.

5 Ladle the soup into glass bowls and add a few ice cubes. Serve garnished with mint, cucumber slices, and whole shrimp.

NUTRITION
Calories *83*; Sugars *7 g*; Protein *12 g*;
Carbohydrate *7 g*; Fat *1 g*; Saturates *0.3 g*

 very easy
3 hrs 30 mins
 0 mins

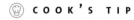 **COOK'S TIP**

Instead of shrimp, add white crab meat or ground chicken. For a vegetarian version of this soup, omit the shrimp and add an extra ¹⁄₃ cup finely diced cucumber. Use fresh vegetable bouillon instead of fish bouillon.

Whole young spinach leaves add vibrant color to this unusual soup. Serve with hot, crusty bread for a nutritious light meal.

Yogurt *and* Spinach Soup

1 Pour the bouillon into a large pan, season, and bring to a boil. Add the rice and simmer for 10 minutes or until barely cooked. Remove from the heat.

2 Combine the water and cornstarch to a smooth paste. Pour the yogurt into a second pan and stir in the cornstarch mixture. Set the pan over a low heat and bring the yogurt to a boil, stirring with a wooden spoon in one direction only. This will stabilize the yogurt and prevent it from separating or curdling on contact with the hot bouillon. When the yogurt has reached boiling point, stand the pan on a heat diffuser and simmer gently for 10 minutes. Remove the pan from the heat and set the mixture aside to cool slightly before stirring in the beaten egg yolks.

3 Pour the yogurt mixture into the bouillon, stir in the lemon juice, and stir to blend thoroughly. Keep the soup warm, but do not allow it to boil.

4 Blanch the washed and drained spinach leaves in a large pan of boiling, salted water for 2-3 minutes or until they begin to soften, but have not wilted. Tip the spinach into a colander, drain well, and stir it into the soup. Warm through. Taste the soup and adjust the seasoning if necessary. Serve immediately in wide shallow soup plates, with hot, fresh crusty bread.

SERVES 4

2½ cups chicken bouillon
4 tbsp long grain rice, rinsed and drained
4 tbsp water
1 tbsp cornstarch
2½ cups lowfat plain yogurt
3 egg yolks, lightly beaten
juice of 1 lemon
12 oz/350 g young spinach leaves, washed and drained
salt and pepper

NUTRITION
Calories 227; Sugars 13 g; Protein 14 g; Carbohydrate 29 g; Fat 7 g; Saturates 2 g

 moderate

 15 mins

 30 mins

This tasty red lentil soup flavored with cilantro is an easy microwave dish. The yogurt adds a light piquancy to the soup.

Red Lentil Soup *with* Yogurt

SERVES 4

2 tbsp butter
1 onion, chopped finely
1 celery stalk, chopped finely
1 large carrot, grated
1 bay leaf
1 cup red lentils
5 cups hot vegetable or chicken bouillon
2 tbsp chopped fresh cilantro
4 tbsp lowfat plain yogurt
salt and pepper
fresh cilantro sprigs, to garnish

1 Place the butter, onion, and celery in a large bowl. Cover and cook in the microwave on High power for 3 minutes.

2 Add the carrot, bay leaf, and lentils. Pour in the bouillon. Cover and cook on High power for 15 minutes, stirring halfway through.

3 Remove the bowl from the microwave oven, cover, and stand for 5 minutes.

4 Remove and discard the bay leaf, then process in batches in a food processor, until smooth. Alternatively, press the soup through a strainer.

5 Pour the soup into a clean bowl. Season with salt and pepper to taste and stir in the cilantro. Cover and cook on High power for 4–5 minutes or until the soup is piping hot.

6 Serve in warmed soup bowls. Stir 1 tablespoon of yogurt into each serving and garnish with small sprigs of fresh cilantro.

NUTRITION
Calories *280*; Sugars *6 g*; Protein *17 g*;
Carbohydrate *40 g*; Fat *7 g*; Saturates *4 g*

 easy

 5 mins

30 mins

 COOK'S TIP

For an extra creamy soup try adding lowfat crème fraîche or sour cream instead of yogurt.

Thai soups are very quickly and easily put together, and are cooked so that each ingredient can still be tasted in the finished dish.

Mushroom *and* Ginger Soup

1 Soak the dried Chinese mushrooms (if using) for at least 30 minutes in 1¼ cups of the hot vegetable bouillon. Remove the stalks and discard, then slice the mushrooms. Reserve the bouillon.

2 Cook the noodles for 2–3 minutes in boiling water. Drain, rinse, and set aside.

3 Heat the oil over high heat in a wok or large, heavy skillet. Add the garlic and ginger, stir, and add the mushrooms. Stir over high heat for 2 minutes.

4 Add the remaining vegetable bouillon with the reserved bouillon and bring to a boil. Add the mushroom catsup and soy sauce.

5 Stir in the beansprouts and cook until tender. Divide the noodles among warmed bowls and ladle the soup on top. Garnish with cilantro leaves and serve immediately.

SERVES 4

½ oz/15 g dried Chinese mushrooms or
    4½ oz/125 g field or cremini mushrooms
4 cups hot vegetable bouillon
4 oz/115 g thread egg noodles
2 tsp sunflower oil
3 garlic cloves, crushed
1-inch/2.5-cm piece gingerroot, shredded
    finely
½ tsp mushroom catsup
1 tsp light soy sauce
1½ cups bean sprouts
cilantro leaves, to garnish

NUTRITION
Calories *74*; Sugars *1 g*; Protein *3 g*;
Carbohydrate *9 g*; Fat *3 g*; Saturates *0.4 g*

 easy

1 hr 30 mins

 15 mins

COOK'S TIP

Rice noodles contain no fat and are ideal for anyone on a lowfat diet.

Carrot soups are very popular and here cumin, tomato, potato, and celery give the soup both richness and depth.

Carrot *and* Cumin Soup

SERVES 4

3 tbsp butter or margarine
1 large onion, chopped
1–2 garlic cloves, crushed
12 oz/350 g carrots, sliced
3¾ cups chicken or vegetable bouillon
¾ tsp ground cumin
2 celery stalks, sliced thinly
4 oz/115 g potato, diced
2 tsp tomato paste
2 tsp lemon juice
2 fresh or dried bay leaves
about 1¼ cups skim milk
salt and pepper
celery leaves, to garnish

1 Melt the butter or margarine in a large pan. Add the onion and garlic and cook very gently until softened.

2 Add the carrots and cook gently for a further 5 minutes, stirring frequently and taking care they do not brown.

3 Add the bouillon, cumin, seasoning, celery, potato, tomato paste, lemon juice, and bay leaves and bring to a boil. Cover and simmer for about 30 minutes or until the vegetables are tender.

4 Remove and discard the bay leaves, cool the soup a little, and then press it through a strainer or process in a food processor or blender until smooth.

5 Pour the soup into a clean pan, add the milk, and bring to a boil over low heat. Taste and adjust the seasoning if necessary.

6 Ladle into warmed bowls and garnish each serving with a small celery leaf. Serve immediately.

NUTRITION
Calories *114*; Sugars *8 g*; Protein *3 g*;
Carbohydrate *12 g*; Fat *6 g*; Saturates *4 g*

 easy

🕐 15 mins

🕐 45 mins

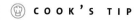 **COOK'S TIP**

This soup can be frozen for up to 3 months. Add the milk when reheating.

A traditional clear soup made from beef bones and lean ground beef. Thin strips of vegetables provide a colourful garnish.

Consommé

1 Put the bouillon and ground beef in a pan. Leave for 1 hour. Add the tomatoes, carrots, onion, celery, turnip (if using), bouquet garni, 2 of the egg whites, the crushed shells of 2 of the eggs, and plenty of seasoning. Bring to almost boiling point, whisking hard all the time with a flat whisk.

2 Cover and simmer for 1 hour, taking care not to allow the layer of froth on top of the soup to break.

3 Pour the soup through a jelly bag or scalded fine cloth, keeping the froth back until the last, then pour the soup through the cloth again into a clean pan. The resulting liquid should be clear.

4 If the soup is not quite clear, return it to the pan with another egg white and the crushed shells of 2 more eggs. Repeat the whisking process as before and then boil for 10 minutes; strain again.

5 Add the sherry (if using) to the soup and reheat gently. Place the garnish in the warmed bowls and carefully pour in the soup. Serve with melba toast.

SERVES 4

5 cups strong Beef Bouillon (see page 15)
1 cup extra lean ground beef
2 tomatoes, peeled, seeded, and chopped
2 large carrots, chopped
1 large onion, chopped
2 celery stalks, chopped
1 turnip, chopped (optional)
1 bouquet garni
2–3 egg whites
shells of 2–4 eggs, crushed
1–2 tbsp sherry (optional)
salt and pepper
melba toast, to serve

to garnish
julienne strips of raw carrot, turnip, celery, or celery root or a one-egg omelet, cut into julienne strips

NUTRITION
Calories *1009*; Sugars *6 g*; Protein *13 g*;
Carbohydrate *7 g*; Fat *3 g*; Saturates *1 g*

✪✪✪✪ challenging
 15 mins
 1 hr 15 mins

Special Occasion

The selection of soups in this chapter offers something a little different. Special occasion soups are appropriate for entertaining, either because of their festive ingredients or their suitability for an informal gathering, or perhaps because they require a little more preparation time than a family dinner normally demands. The cold soups included in this chapter are also for special occasions and home entertainment, and are equally welcome on a hot summer's day as a refreshing treat.

This is a classic combination of ingredients all brought together in a delicious, creamy soup. Serve with whole-wheat bread for a light lunch.

Stilton *and* Walnut Soup

SERVES 4

4 tbsp butter
2 shallots, chopped
3 celery stalks, chopped
1 garlic clove, chopped finely
2 tbsp all-purpose flour
2½ cups vegetable bouillon
1¼ cups milk
1½ cups crumbled blue Stilton cheese,
    plus extra to garnish
2 tbsp walnut halves, chopped roughly
⅔ cup plain yogurt
salt and pepper
chopped celery leaves, to garnish

1 Melt the butter in a large, heavy pan and cook the shallots, celery, and garlic for 2–3 minutes, stirring, until soft.

2 Lower the heat, add the flour, and cook, stirring, for 30 seconds.

3 Gradually stir in the vegetable bouillon and milk and bring to a boil.

4 Reduce the heat to a simmer and add the crumbled blue Stilton cheese and walnut halves. Cover and simmer for 20 minutes.

5 Stir in the plain yogurt and heat for a further 2 minutes without boiling.

6 Season the soup, then transfer to a warmed soup tureen or individual serving bowls.

7 Garnish the soup with the chopped celery leaves and extra crumbled blue Stilton cheese, and serve immediately.

NUTRITION
Calories *392*; Sugars *8 g*; Protein *15 g*;
Carbohydrate *15 g*; Fat *30 g*; Saturates *16 g*

 very easy

 10 mins

30 mins

🍳 **COOK'S TIP**

As well as adding protein, vitamins, and useful fats to the diet, nuts add important flavor and texture to vegetarian meals.

Ground almonds add valuable protein and a rich, luxurious depth to this delicately colored soup.

Carrot *and* Almond Soup

1 Heat the oil in a large pan over a medium heat and add the onion and leek. Cover and cook for about 3 minutes, stirring occasionally, until just soft; do not let them brown.

2 Add the carrots and water and season with a little salt and pepper. Bring to a boil, reduce the heat, and simmer gently, partially covered, for about 45 minutes or until the vegetables are tender. Remove from the heat.

3 Soak the bread crumbs in cold water to cover for 2–3 minutes, then strain them and press out the remaining water.

4 Put the almonds and bread crumbs in a blender or food processor with a ladleful of the carrot cooking water and purée until smooth and paste-like.

5 Transfer the soup vegetables and remaining cooking liquid to the blender or food processor and purée until smooth, working in batches if necessary. (If using a food processor, strain off the cooking liquid and reserve. Purée the soup solids with enough cooking liquid to moisten them, then combine with the remaining liquid.)

6 Return the soup to the pan and simmer over low heat, stirring occasionally, until heated through. Add lemon juice, salt, and pepper to taste.

7 Ladle the soup into warmed bowls, garnish with chives, and serve.

SERVES 4

2 tsp olive oil
1 onion, chopped finely
1 leek, sliced thinly
4 cups thinly sliced carrots
6¼ cups water
1 cup loosely packed soft white bread crumbs
1½ cups ground almonds
1 tbsp fresh lemon juice, or to taste
salt and pepper
snipped fresh chives, to garnish

NUTRITION
Calories 275; Sugars 10 g; Protein 9 g;
Carbohydrate 16 g; Fat 20 g; Saturates 2 g

✪✪✪ moderate
 15 mins
 55 mins

A rich and creamy pale green soup made with avocados and enhanced by a touch of chopped mint. Serve chilled in summer or hot in winter.

Avocado *and* Mint Soup

SERVES 6

3 tbsp butter or margarine
6 scallions, sliced
1 garlic clove, crushed
¼ cup all-purpose flour
2½ cups vegetable bouillon
2 ripe avocados
2–3 tsp lemon juice
pinch of grated lemon zest
⅔ cup milk
⅔ cup light cream
1–1½ tbsp chopped mint
salt and pepper
mint sprigs, to garnish

minted garlic bread
½ cup butter
1–2 tbsp chopped mint
1–2 garlic cloves, crushed
1 whole wheat or white French bread stick

NUTRITION
Calories *199*; Sugars *3 g*; Protein *3 g*;
Carbohydrate *7 g*; Fat *18 g*; Saturates *6 g*

 very easy

 15 mins

15 mins

35 mins

1 Melt the butter or margarine in a large, heavy-based pan. Add the scallions and garlic clove and cook over a low heat, stirring occasionally, for about 3 minutes or until soft and translucent.

2 Stir in the flour and cook, stirring, for 1–2 minutes. Gradually stir in the bouillon, then bring to a boil. Simmer gently while preparing the avocados.

3 Peel the avocados, discard the pits, and chop coarsely. Add to the soup with the lemon juice and zest and seasoning. Cover and simmer for about 10 minutes or until tender.

4 Cool the soup slightly, then press through a strainer with the back of a spoon or process in a food processor or blender until a smooth purée forms. Pour into a bowl.

5 Stir in the milk and cream, adjust the seasoning, then stir in the mint. Cover and chill thoroughly.

6 To make the minted garlic bread, soften the butter and beat in the mint and garlic. Cut the loaf into slanting slices but leave a hinge on the bottom crust. Spread each slice with the butter and reassemble the loaf. Wrap in foil and place in a preheated oven, 350°F/180°C, for about 15 minutes.

7 Serve the soup garnished with a sprig of mint and accompanied by the minted garlic bread.

This rich and elegant soup is the perfect start for a special dinner. The lobster shell, made into a bouillon, contributes greatly to the flavor of the soup.

Lobster Bisque

1 Pull off the lobster tail. With the legs up, cut the body in half lengthways. Scoop out the tomalley (the soft pale greenish-gray part) and, if it is a female, the roe (the solid red-orange part). Reserve these together, covered and refrigerated. Remove the meat and cut into bite-sized pieces; cover and refrigerate. Chop the shell into large pieces.

2 Melt half the butter in a large pan over a medium heat and add the lobster shell. Cook until brown bits begin to stick on the bottom of the pan. Add the carrot, celery, leek, onion, and shallots. Cook, stirring, for 1½–2 minutes (do not let it burn). Add the alcohol and bubble for 1 minute. Pour over the water, add the tomato paste, a large pinch of salt and bring to a boil. Reduce the heat, simmer for 30 minutes, and strain the bouillon, discarding the solids.

3 Melt the remaining butter in a small pan and add the tomalley and roe, if any. Add the cream, whisk well, remove from the heat, and set aside.

4 Put the flour in a small bowl and very slowly whisk in 2–3 tablespoons of cold water. Stir in a little of the hot bouillon to make a smooth liquid.

5 Bring the remaining bouillon to a boil and whisk in the flour mixture. Simmer for 4–5 minutes until the soup thickens, stirring frequently. Press the tomalley mixture through a strainer into the soup. Reduce the heat and add the reserved lobster meat. Simmer until heated through.

6 Taste the soup and adjust the seasoning, adding more cream if wished. Ladle into warmed bowls, sprinkle with chives, and serve.

SERVES 4

1 lb/450 g cooked lobster
3 tbsp butter
1 small carrot, grated
1 celery stalk, chopped finely
1 leek, chopped finely
1 small onion, chopped finely
2 shallots, chopped finely
3 tbsp brandy or Cognac
¼ cup dry white wine
5 cups water
1 tbsp tomato paste
½ cup whipping cream, or to taste
6 tbsp all-purpose flour
salt and pepper
snipped fresh chives, to garnish

NUTRITION

Calories *398*; Sugars *6 g*; Protein *14 g*; Carbohydrate *30 g*; Fat *22 g*; Saturates *14 g*

 moderate

20 mins

50 mins

This soup makes a rich and elegant starter. Serve it in shallow bowls so the oysters are visible, and make sure you warm the bowls to keep the soup hot.

Creamy Oyster Soup

SERVES 4

12 oysters
2 tbsp butter
2 shallots, chopped finely
5 tbsp white wine
1¼ cups fish bouillon
¾ cup whipping or heavy cream
2 tbsp cornstarch, dissolved in 2 tbsp
   cold water
salt and pepper
caviar or lumpfish roe, to garnish (optional)

NUTRITION
Calories *299*; Sugars *3 g*; Protein *3 g*;
Carbohydrate *16 g*; Fat *24 g*; Saturates *15 g*

easy

20 mins

30 mins

1 To open the oysters, hold flat-side up, over a strainer set over a bowl to catch the juices, and push an oyster knife into the hinge. Work it around until you can pry off the top shell. When all the oysters have been opened, strain the liquid through a strainer lined with damp cheesecloth. Remove any bits of shell stuck to the oysters and reserve them in their liquid.

2 Melt half the butter in a pan over a low heat. Add the shallots and cook gently for about 5 minutes or until just softened, stirring frequently; do not allow them to brown.

3 Add the wine, bring to a boil, and boil for 1 minute. Stir in the fish bouillon, bring back to a boil, and boil for 3–4 minutes. Reduce the heat to a gentle simmer.

4 Add the oysters and their liquid and poach for about 1 minute or until they become more firm but are still tender. Remove the oysters with a slotted spoon and reserve, covered. Strain the bouillon.

5 Bring the strained bouillon to a boil in a clean pan. Add the cream and bring back to a boil.

6 Stir the dissolved cornstarch into the soup and boil gently for 2–3 minutes, stirring frequently, until slightly thickened. Add the oysters and cook for 1–2 minutes to reheat them. Taste and adjust the seasoning, if necessary, and ladle the soup into warmed bowls. Top each serving with a teaspoon of caviar or roe, if using.

This world-famous French soup makes a festive seafood extravaganza worthy of any special occasion or celebration.

Bouillabaisse

1 Peel the shrimp and reserve the shells. Cut the fish fillets into serving pieces about 2 inches/5 cm square. Trim off any ragged edges and reserve. Put the fish in a bowl with 2 tablespoons of the olive oil, the orange zest, 1 garlic clove, finely chopped, and chili paste. Turn to coat well, cover, and chill the shrimp and fish separately.

2 Heat 1 tablespoon of the olive oil in a large pan over medium heat. Add the leek, 1 onion, sliced, and red bell pepper. Cover and cook for 5 minutes, stirring, until the onion softens. Slice the remaining garlic and stir in with the tomatoes, bay leaf, saffron, fennel seeds, shrimp shells, fish trimmings, water, and fish bouillon. Bring to a boil, then simmer, covered, for 30 minutes. Strain the bouillon.

3 Heat the remaining oil in a large pan. Add the fennel and remaining onion, chopped, and cook for 5 minutes, stirring, until softened. Add the bouillon and potatoes and bring to a boil. Reduce the heat slightly, cover, and cook for 12–15 minutes or until just tender.

4 Reduce the heat and add the fish, thick pieces first and thinner ones after 2–3 minutes. Add the shrimp and scallops and simmer until all the seafood is cooked and opaque throughout.

5 Taste the soup and adjust the seasoning. Ladle into warmed bowls. Spread the aïoli sauce on the toasted bread slices and arrange on top of the soup.

SERVES 6

1 lb/450 g jumbo shrimp
1 lb 10 oz/750 g firm white fish fillets, such as sea bass, snapper, and monkfish
4 tbsp olive oil
grated zest of 1 orange
5 large garlic cloves
1/2 tsp chili paste or harissa
1 large leek, sliced
2 onions
1 red bell pepper, seeded and sliced
3–4 tomatoes, cored and cut into 8 wedges
1 bay leaf
pinch of saffron threads
1/2 tsp fennel seeds
2 1/2 cups water
5 cups fish bouillon
1 fennel bulb, chopped finely
8 oz/225 g potatoes, halved and thinly sliced
9 oz/250 g scallops
salt and pepper
toasted French bread slices and ready-prepared aïoli, to serve

NUTRITION
Calories 55; Sugars 1.1 g; Protein 7.2 g; Carbohydrate 2.6 g; Fat 1.8 g; Saturates 0.3 g

easy
10 mins
1 hr

This tomato-based Californian soup is brimming with seafood, which can be varied according to availability. Serve it with olive bread or ciabatta.

Cioppino

SERVES 4

1 lb 2 oz/500 g mussels
1 lb 2 oz/500 g clams, rinsed
1¼ cups dry white wine
1 tbsp olive oil
1 large onion, chopped finely
1 celery stalk, chopped finely
1 yellow or green bell pepper, cored, seeded, and finely chopped
14 oz/400 g canned chopped tomatoes juice
3 garlic cloves, chopped very finely
1 tbsp tomato paste
1 bay leaf
1½ cups fish bouillon or water
6 oz/175 g small squid, cleaned and cut into small pieces
8 oz/225 g skinless white fish fillets, such as cod, sole, or haddock
5½ oz/150 g small scallops, or cooked shelled shrimp
chopped fresh parsley, to garnish

NUTRITION

Calories *211*; Sugars *7 g*; Protein *26 g*;
Carbohydrate *10 g*; Fat *4 g*; Saturates *1 g*

 moderate

 20 mins

1 hr 15 mins

1 Discard any broken or open mussels. Rinse, pull off any "beards", and if there are barnacles, scrape them with a knife under cold water. Put the mussels in a large heavy-based pan. Cover tightly and cook over a high heat for about 4 minutes or until the mussels open, shaking the pan occasionally.

2 Remove the mussels from the shells, adding any juices to the cooking liquid. Strain the cooking liquid through a cheesecloth-lined strainer and reserve.

3 Put the clams into a heavy pan with ¼ cup of the wine. Cover tightly, place over a medium-high heat and cook for 2–4 minutes or until they open. Remove the clams from the shells and strain the cooking liquid through a cheesecloth-lined strainer and reserve.

4 Heat the olive oil in a large pan over a medium-low heat. Add the onion, celery, and bell pepper and cook for 3–4 minutes or until the onion softens, stirring occasionally. Add the remaining wine, tomatoes, garlic, tomato paste, and bay leaf. Continue cooking for 10 minutes.

5 Stir in the fish bouillon or water, squid, and reserved mussel and clam cooking liquids. Bring to a boil, reduce the heat, and simmer for 35–40 minutes or until the vegetables and squid are tender.

6 Add the fish, mussels, and clams and simmer, stirring occasionally, for about 4 minutes or until the fish becomes opaque. Stir in the scallops and continue simmering for 3–4 minutes or until heated through. Remove the bay leaf, ladle into warmed bowls, and sprinkle with chopped parsley.

This lean, pretty soup makes an elegant light entrée for 4 or it will serve 6 as an appetizer. Last-minute assembly is needed, but it's worth it.

Beef *and* Spring Vegetable Soup

1 Bring a pan of lightly salted water to a boil and add the potatoes and carrots. Reduce the heat, cover, and boil gently for about 15 minutes or until tender. Bring another pan of lightly salted water to a boil, add the beans, and boil for about 5 minutes or until just tender. Drain the vegetables and reserve.

2 Bring the bouillon to a boil in a pan and add the soy sauce and sherry. Season with salt and pepper. Reduce the heat, add the beef, and simmer gently for 10 minutes. (The beef should be very rare, as it will continue cooking in the bowls.)

3 Add the mushrooms and simmer for a further 3 minutes. Warm the bowls in a low oven.

4 Remove the meat and set aside to rest on a carving board. Taste the bouillon and adjust the seasoning, if necessary. Bring the bouillon back to a boil.

5 Cut the meat in half lengthwise and slice each half into pieces about ⅛ inch/3 mm thick. Season the meat lightly with salt and pepper and divide among the warmed bowls.

6 Drop the reserved vegetables into the bouillon and heat through for about 1 minute. Ladle the bouillon over the meat, dividing the vegetables as evenly as possible. Sprinkle over the parsley and chives and serve immediately.

SERVES 4 – 6

12 small new potatoes, quartered

4 slim carrots, quartered lengthwise and cut into 1½-inch/4-cm lengths

5½ oz/150 g tiny green beans, cut into 1½ inch/4 cm lengths

6¾ cups rich beef or meat bouillon

2 tbsp soy sauce

3 tbsp dry sherry

12 oz/350 g beef tenderloin, about 2 inches/5 cm thick

2¼ cups sliced shiitake mushrooms

1 tbsp chopped fresh parsley

1 tbsp chopped fresh chives

salt and pepper

NUTRITION

Calories *166*; Sugars *3 g*; Protein *16 g*; Carbohydrate *17 g*; Fat *4 g*; Saturates *1 g*

  moderate

15–20 mins

35 mins

This soup needs a rich bouillon, and the mushrooms contribute plenty of extra flavor. The pastry top is baked separately to simplify serving the dish.

Chicken *and* Mushroom Soup

SERVES 6

7 cups chicken bouillon
4 skinless boneless chicken breasts
2 garlic cloves, crushed
small bunch of fresh tarragon or ¼ tsp
   dried tarragon
1 tbsp butter
14 oz/400 g cremini or horse mushrooms,
   sliced
3 tbsp dry white wine
6 tbsp all-purpose flour
¾ cup whipping or heavy cream
13 oz/375 g puff pastry
2 tbsp finely chopped fresh parsley
salt and pepper

1 Put the bouillon in a pan and bring just to a boil. Add the chicken, garlic, and tarragon, reduce the heat, then cover and simmer for 20 minutes or until the chicken is cooked through. Remove the chicken and strain the bouillon. When the chicken is cool, cut into bite-sized pieces.

2 Melt the butter in a large skillet over a medium heat. Add the mushrooms and season. Cook for 5–8 minutes or until they are golden brown, stirring occasionally at first, then stirring more often after they start to color. Add the wine and bubble briefly. Remove the mushrooms from the heat.

3 Put the flour in a small mixing bowl and very slowly whisk in the cream to make a thick paste. Stir in a little of the bouillon to make a smooth liquid.

4 Bring the strained bouillon to a boil in a large pan. Whisk in the flour mixture and bring back to a boil. Boil gently for 3–4 minutes or until the soup thickens, stirring frequently. Add the cooked mushrooms and liquid, if any. Reduce the heat to low and simmer very gently, just to keep warm.

5 Cut out 6 rounds of pastry smaller in diameter than the soup bowls, using a plate as a guide. Put on a cookie sheet, prick with a fork, and bake in a preheated oven at 400°F/200°C for about 15 minutes or until deep golden.

6 Meanwhile, add the chicken to the soup. Taste and adjust the seasoning. Simmer for about 10 minutes or until heated through. Stir in the parsley. Ladle the soup into warmed bowls and place the pastry rounds on top. Serve immediately.

NUTRITION

Calories *513*; Sugars *2 g*; Protein *28 g*;
Carbohydrate *44 g*; Fat *33 g*; Saturates *10 g*

moderate

15 mins

50 mins

This an excellent soup to serve during the fall, when pheasant are more widely available.

Pheasant Soup *with* Cider

1 Melt half of the butter in a large pan over a medium heat. Add the shallots and garlic and cook for 3–4 minutes or until softened. Pour over the cider and bring to a boil. Add the bouillon, carrot, celery, bay leaf, and pheasant, which should be submerged. Bring back to a boil, reduce the heat, cover, and simmer for about 1 hour or until the pheasant is very tender.

2 Remove the meat from the bones and cut into bite-sized pieces. Strain the bouillon, pressing with the back of a spoon to extract all the liquid. Discard the vegetables and bay leaf and remove as much fat as possible.

3 Bring the bouillon to a boil in a large pan. Simmer very gently. Cook the potatoes for 15 minutes or until they are just barely tender.

4 Meanwhile, melt the remaining butter in a large skillet over a medium heat. Add the mushrooms and season with salt and pepper. Cook for 5–8 minutes, until they are golden brown, stirring on occasion, then more often once they start to change colour.

5 Add the mushrooms to the soup, with the apple and cream, and cook for about 10 minutes or until the apple and potatoes are tender. Whisk in the diluted cornstarch. Boil gently for 2–3 minutes, whisking, until slightly thickened. Add the pheasant meat and simmer gently until the soup is hot.

6 Heat the oil in a small skillet until it starts to smoke. Add the sage leaves and fry for about 20 seconds or until crispy. Drain on paper towels. Ladle the soup into warmed bowls and garnish with fried sage.

SERVES 4

2 tbsp butter
3 shallots, chopped finely
2 garlic cloves, sliced thinly
1¼ cups hard cider
5 cups pheasant or chicken bouillon
1 carrot, chopped finely
1 celery stalk, chopped finely
1 bay leaf
1 pheasant
10½ oz/300 g potatoes, diced
9 oz/250 g small button mushrooms, halved or quartered
1 large eating apple, peeled and diced
1¼ cups heavy cream
4 tbsp cornstarch, diluted with 3 tbsp cold water
salt and pepper

to garnish
2 tbsp olive oil, or as needed
30 sage leaves

NUTRITION
Calories *471*; Sugars *8 g*; Protein *12 g*; Carbohydrate *32 g*; Fat *32 g*; Saturates *19 g*

⊛⊛⊛   moderate

🕐   30 mins

🕐   1 hr 45 mins

If you can't find the preserved duck or goose (confit) that is traditionally used for this dish, you could braise duck legs in bouillon or substitute smoked chicken, but it will be a different soup.

Duck, Cabbage, *and* Bean Soup

SERVES 6

2 preserved duck legs
1 tbsp duck fat or olive oil
1 onion, chopped finely
4 garlic cloves, chopped finely
2 carrots, sliced
1 large leek, halved lengthways and sliced
2 turnips, diced
7 oz/200 g dark leafy cabbage, such as cavolo nero or Savoy
5 cups chicken or duck bouillon
2 potatoes, diced
8 oz/225 g dried white beans, soaked and cooked, or 28 oz/800 g canned white beans
1 bay leaf
2 tbsp roughly chopped fresh parsley
12 slices baguette
5½ oz/150 g grated Gruyére cheese
salt and pepper

NUTRITION
Calories *479*; Sugars *8 g*; Protein *29 g*; Carbohydrate *57 g*; Fat *16 g*; Saturates *7 g*

easy

20 mins

1 hr 15 mins

1 Scrape as much fat as possible from the preserved duck. Remove the duck meat from the bones, keeping it in large pieces; discard the skin and bones.

2 Heat the duck fat or olive oil in a large soup kettle or flameproof casserole over a medium heat. Add the onion and three-quarters of the garlic. Cover and cook for 3–4 minutes or until just softened. Add the carrots, leek, and turnips, cover and continue cooking for 20 minutes, stirring occasionally. If the vegetables start to brown, add a tablespoon of water.

3 Meanwhile, bring a large pan of salted water to a boil. Drop in the cabbage and boil gently for 5 minutes. Drain well.

4 Add the bouillon to the stewed vegetables. Stir in the potatoes, beans, parboiled cabbage, and bay leaf, adjust seasoning. Bring almost to a boil, reduce the heat, and simmer for 15 minutes.

5 Chop together the parsley and remaining garlic. Stir into the soup with the preserved duck, cover again, and simmer for about 20 minutes, stirring occasionally. Season to taste.

6 Toast the bread under a preheated hot broiler on one side. Turn and top with the cheese. Broil until the cheese melts. Ladle the soup into warmed bowls and top with the cheese toasts.

This delicious soup has a rich homemade Italian-style meat bouillon as a base. A perfect dinner party starter, it is very light —and easy to make if you have a supply of the bouillon in the freezer.

Parmesan Cheese Pancakes *in* Broth

1 To make the bouillon, put the chicken and beef in a large pot with the water, celery, carrot, onion, garlic, parsley stems, bay leaf, and salt. Bring just to a boil and skim off the foam that rises to the surface. Reduce the heat and simmer very gently, uncovered, for 2 hours.

2 Strain the bouillon and remove as much fat as possible. Discard the vegetables and herbs. (Save the meat for another purpose.)

3 Bring the bouillon to a boil in a clean pan. If necessary, boil to reduce the bouillon to 4 cups. Taste and adjust the seasoning (be restrained with salt). Reduce the heat and simmer gently while making the pancakes.

4 To make the pancakes, put the flour in a bowl and add half the milk. Whisk until smooth, add the remaining milk, and whisk again. Break in the eggs and whisk to combine well. Season and stir in the basil and Parmesan.

5 Brush the bottom of a small non-stick 6–7-inch/15–18-cm skillet with oil and heat until it begins to smoke. Pour in one-third of the batter (about 4 tablespoons) and tilt the pan so the batter covers the bottom. Cook for about 1 minute or until mostly set around the edges. Turn the pancake and cook the other side for about 15 seconds. Turn out on to a plate. Continue making the remaining pancakes, adding more oil to the pan if needed.

6 Roll the pancakes up while warm, then cut into ⅛-inch/3-mm slices across the roll to make spirals. Divide the pancake spirals among bowls. Ladle over the hot broth and serve with Parmesan.

SERVES 4

1 tbsp all-purpose flour
2 tbsp milk
2 eggs
2 tbsp chopped fresh basil
3 tbsp freshly grated Parmesan cheese, plus extra to serve

meat bouillon
1 lb/450 g chicken wings and/or legs
9 oz/250 g lean boneless stewing beef, such as shin
6 cups water
1 celery stalk, sliced thinly
1 carrot, sliced thinly
1 onion, halved and sliced
2 garlic cloves, crushed
3–4 parsley stems
1 bay leaf
½ tsp salt
pepper

NUTRITION
Calories 37; Sugars 0 g; Protein 9 g; Carbohydrate 3 g; Fat 2 g; Saturates 1 g

 moderate

 25 mins

2 hrs 30 mins

Jerusalem artichokes are curious to look at but make a very tasty and satisfying winter soup.

Jerusalem Artichoke *and* Swede Soup

SERVES 6

1 lb/450 g Jerusalem artichokes
2 tsp butter
1 onion, chopped finely
½ cup peeled and cubed rutabaga
1 strip pared lemon zest
3 cups vegetable bouillon
3 tbsp heavy cream
1 tbsp fresh lemon juice, or to taste
4 tbsp lightly toasted pine nuts

1 Peel the Jerusalem artichokes and cut large ones into pieces. Drop the artichokes into a bowl of cold water to prevent discoloration.

2 Melt the butter in a large pan over medium heat. Add the onion and cook for about 3 minutes, stirring frequently, until just soft.

3 Drain the Jerusalem artichokes and add them to the pan with the rutabaga and lemon zest. Pour in the bouillon, season with a little salt and pepper, and stir to combine. Bring just to a boil, reduce the heat, and simmer gently for about 20 minutes or until the vegetables are tender.

4 Let the soup cool slightly, then transfer to a blender or food processor and purée until smooth. (If using a food processor, strain off the cooking liquid and reserve. Purée the soup solids with just enough cooking liquid to moisten them, then combine with the remaining liquid.)

5 Return the soup to the pan, stir in the cream, and simmer for about 5 minutes until reheated. Add the lemon juice. Taste and adjust the seasoning, adding more lemon juice if wished. Ladle the soup into warmed bowls and very gently place the pine nuts on top, dividing them evenly. Serve at once.

NUTRITION
Calories *285*; Sugars *5 g*; Protein *5 g*;
Carbohydrate *16 g*; Fat *24 g*; Saturates *9 g*

  moderate

  20 mins

20 mins

30 mins

The combination of potato, garlic, and onion works marvelously in soup. In this recipe the garlic is roasted to give it added dimension and depth.

Garlic *and* Potato Soup

1 Put the garlic cloves in a baking dish. Lightly brush with oil and bake in a preheated oven at 350°F/180°C for about 20 minutes or until golden.

2 Heat the oil in a large pan over medium heat. Add the leeks and onion, then cover and cook for about 3 minutes, stirring frequently, until just soft.

3 Add the potatoes, roasted garlic, bouillon, and bay leaf. Season with salt (unless the bouillon is salty) and pepper. Bring to a boil, then reduce the heat, cover, and cook gently for about 30 minutes or until the vegetables are tender. Remove the bay leaf.

4 Let the soup cool slightly, then transfer to a blender or food processor and purée until smooth, working in batches if necessary. (If using a food processor, strain off the cooking liquid and reserve. Purée the soup solids with enough cooking liquid to moisten them, then combine with the remaining liquid.)

5 Return the soup to the pan and stir in the cream and a generous grating of nutmeg. Taste and adjust the seasoning, if necessary, adding a few drops of lemon juice, if wished. Reheat over low heat. Ladle into warmed soup bowls, then garnish with chives or parsley and serve.

SERVES 4

1 large bulb garlic with large cloves, peeled (about 4 oz/115 g)
2 tsp olive oil
2 large leeks, sliced thinly
1 large onion, chopped finely
2¾ cups diced potatoes
5 cups vegetable bouillon
1 bay leaf
⅔ cup light cream
freshly grated nutmeg
fresh lemon juice, optional
salt and pepper
snipped fresh chives, to garnish

NUTRITION
Calories *240*; Sugars *7 g*; Protein *8 g*; Carbohydrate *33 g*; Fat *10 g*; Saturates *5 g*

 moderate

 10 mins

1 hr

When cucumber is cooked it becomes a much more subtle vegetable, perfect to set off the taste of smoked salmon. This cold soup makes a lovely starter.

Cucumber *and* Smoked Salmon Soup

SERVES 4

2 tsp oil
1 large onion, chopped finely
1 large cucumber, peeled, seeded, and sliced
1 small potato, diced
1 celery stalk, chopped finely
4 cups chicken or vegetable bouillon
²⁄₃ cup heavy cream
5½ oz/150 g smoked salmon, diced finely
2 tbsp chopped fresh chives
salt and pepper
fresh dill sprigs, to garnish

1 Heat the oil in a large pan over a medium heat. Add the onion and cook for about 3 minutes or until it begins to soften.

2 Add the cucumber, potato, celery, and bouillon, along with a large pinch of salt, if using unsalted bouillon. Bring to a boil, reduce the heat, cover, and cook gently for about 20 minutes or until the vegetables are tender.

3 Allow the soup to cool slightly, then transfer to a blender or food processor, working in batches if necessary.

4 Purée the soup until smooth. If using a food processor, strain off the cooking liquid and reserve it. Purée the soup solids with enough cooking liquid to moisten them, then combine with the remaining liquid.

5 Transfer the soup into a large container. Cover and refrigerate until cold.

6 Stir the cream, salmon, and chives into the soup. If time permits, chill for at least 1 hour to allow the flavors to blend. Taste and adjust the seasoning, adding salt, if needed, and pepper. Ladle into chilled bowls and garnish with fresh sprigs of dill.

NUTRITION
Calories *308*; Sugars *7 g*; Protein *13 g*;
Carbohydrate *15 g*; Fat *22 g*; Saturates *12 g*

   easy

   15 mins

15 mins

25 mins

This brilliantly colored soup makes a great summer starter, especially when bell peppers are abundant in farm markets—or in your garden.

Spicy Red Pepper Soup

1 Heat the oil in a large pan over medium heat. Add the leeks, onion, and garlic and cook, stirring occasionally, for 5 minutes or until the onion is softened.

2 Stir in the bell peppers and cook for a further 2–3 minutes. Add the water, cumin, ground coriander, and chili paste with a pinch of salt. Bring to a boil, reduce the heat, cover, and simmer gently for about 35 minutes or until all the vegetables are tender.

3 Set aside to cool slightly, then transfer to a blender or food processor, and process to a smooth purée, in batches if necessary. (If using a food processor, strain off the cooking liquid and reserve. Purée the soup solids with enough cooking liquid to moisten them, then combine with the remaining liquid.)

4 Put the soup in a large bowl, then season with salt and pepper, and add lemon juice to taste. Allow to cool completely, cover with plastic wrap, and chill in the refrigerator until cold.

5 Before serving, taste and adjust the seasoning, if necessary. Add a little more chili paste if a spicy taste is preferred. Ladle into chilled bowls and garnish with scallion greens or chives.

SERVES 6

1 tbsp olive oil
1 lb/450 g leeks, sliced thinly
1 large onion, halved and thinly sliced
2 garlic cloves, chopped finely or crushed
6 red bell peppers, seeded and sliced
4 cups water
½ tsp ground cumin
½ tsp ground coriander
1 tsp chili paste
1–2 tsp fresh lemon juice
salt and pepper
finely chopped scallion greens or fresh chives, to garnish

NUTRITION

Calories *90*; Sugars *13 g*; Protein *3 g*; Carbohydrate *15 g*; Fat *3 g*; Saturates *0 g*

★★★ moderate

 45 mins

 45 mins

The zingy hot taste of fresh ginger blends perfectly with cool melon in this intriguing soup.

Melon *and* Ginger Soup

SERVES 4

1 large ripe melon (about 2 lb/900 g)
¾ tsp grated peeled fresh gingerroot, or more to taste
1 tbsp fresh lemon juice, or to taste
1 tsp sugar
½ cup whipping cream
salt
snipped fresh chives, to garnish

1 Halve the melon, discard the seeds, and scoop the flesh into a blender or food processor. Purée until smooth, scraping down the sides as necessary. (You may need to work in batches.)

2 Add the grated ginger, lemon juice, and sugar, with a pinch of salt and process to combine. Taste and add a little more ginger, if desired. Scrape into a bowl, cover, and chill completely, usually for about 30 minutes or until cold.

3 Add the cream and stir to combine well. Taste and adjust the seasoning, adding a little more salt and lemon juice if necessary.

4 To serve, divide the melon purée among four chilled bowls and garnish with chives.

NUTRITION
Calories *176*; Sugars *16 g*; Protein *2 g*;
Carbohydrate *16 g*; Fat *12 g*; Saturates *7 g*

★★★   moderate
   15 mins
   0 mins

🍲 COOK'S TIP

To determine the ripeness of melon, gently press the end opposite the stem— it should give a little, and there is usually a characteristic aroma on pressing that helps to confirm that it is ripe.

This soup brings together Thai flavors for a cool, refreshing appetizer. It highlights fresh cilantro, now more widely available.

Cold Cilantro Soup

1 Heat the oil in a large pan over medium heat. Add the onion, leek, and garlic and cook, stirring occasionally, for 4–5 minutes or until the onion is soft, but not browned.

2 Add the water, zucchini, and rice with a pinch of salt and some pepper. Stir in the lemon grass and lime leaves. Bring just to a boil and reduce the heat to low. Cover and simmer for 15–20 minutes or until the rice is soft and tender.

3 Add the fresh cilantro leaves and stems, pushing them down into the liquid. Continue cooking over low heat for 2–3 minutes or until the leaves are wilted. Remove and discard the lemon grass and lime leaves.

4 Remove from the heat and let cool slightly, then transfer to a blender or food processor, and process to a smooth purée, working in batches if necessary. (If using a food processor, strain off the cooking liquid and reserve. Purée the soup solids with enough cooking liquid to moisten them, then combine with the remaining liquid.)

5 Scrape the soup into a large container. Season to taste with salt and pepper. Cover with plastic wrap and chill in the refrigerator until cold.

6 Taste and adjust the seasoning. For a spicier soup, stir in a little chili paste to taste. For a thinner soup, add a small amount of ice water. Ladle into chilled bowls and garnish with finely chopped red bell pepper and/or chiles.

SERVES 4

2 tsp olive oil
1 large onion, chopped finely
1 leek, sliced thinly
1 garlic clove, sliced thinly
4 cups water
1 zucchini, about 7 oz/200 g, peeled and chopped
4 tbsp long grain white rice
2-inch/5-cm piece of lemon grass
2 lime leaves
2 cups fresh cilantro leaves and soft stems
chili paste, optional
salt and pepper
finely chopped red bell pepper and/or fresh red chiles, to garnish

NUTRITION
Calories 79; Sugars 5 g; Protein 3 g;
Carbohydrate 13 g; Fat 3 g; Saturates 0 g

easy

45 mins

30 mins

Index